The Cambridge Manuals of Science and
Literature

GOETHE
AND THE TWENTIETH CENTURY

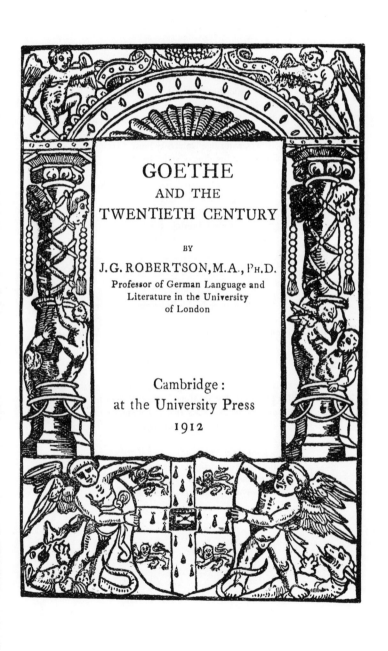

GOETHE
AND THE
TWENTIETH CENTURY

BY

J. G. ROBERTSON, M.A., PH.D.

Professor of German Language and
Literature in the University
of London

Cambridge:
at the University Press

1912

CAMBRIDGE UNIVERSITY PRESS
Cambridge, New York, Melbourne, Madrid, Cape Town,
Singapore, São Paulo, Delhi, Tokyo, Mexico City

Cambridge University Press
The Edinburgh Building, Cambridge CB2 8RU, UK

Published in the United States of America by
Cambridge University Press, New York

www.cambridge.org
Information on this title: www.cambridge.org/9781107401853

© Cambridge University Press 1912

First published 1912
First paperback edition 2011

A catalogue record for this publication is available from the British Library

ISBN 978-1-107-40185-3 Paperback

*With the exception of the coat of arms
at the foot, the design on the title page is a
reproduction of one used by the earliest known
Cambridge printer, John Siberch, 1521*

PREFACE

GOETHE is one of those chameleon-like personalities that change in value and meaning from generation to generation. Homer, Dante, Shakespeare have been given, once and for all, their place in the world's literature, and what we think about them to-day is not materially different from what our forefathers thought; but then those poets are, in comparison, infinitely far away from us; Goethe still stands too near. We must revise our opinion of him from time to time: keep, as it were, a check on the pulse of our intellectual attitude to him. And this revision of judgment is something which we must do for ourselves. Germany, for the past five and twenty years at least, has been assiduously remoulding her literary opinions, and has progressed very far indeed from the old Hegelian self-satisfaction with which she established the hierarchy of her classical poets about the middle of the past century. But we obviously cannot rely on Germany for our opinions of Goethe, any more than Germany can turn to us to find what she has to think about English poets. Learn from her we can; we cannot afford to let anything escape us of that vast treasure of carefully garnered fact and scholarly inference which her best minds, with amazing industry, have been accumulating in recent years. But the actual judgment, the estimating of values—that we must do for ourselves, if it is to have a vital meaning for us. When a poet is great enough to interest a nation beyond his own, that nation must perforce weigh him by its own standards, must see him from the national angle.

Moreover, in the case of a poet like Goethe this necessity of independent judgment is peculiarly urgent. For Goethe has passed so completely into the flesh and blood of the modern German that the latter's attitude to him is difficult for us to comprehend unless we possess a rare familiarity with contemporary modes of German thought. The intellectual fabric of modern Germany is built on and round Goethe : it cannot dissociate itself from Goethe ; Goethe has defined its horizons. We Anglo-Saxons, on the other hand, are, in respect of Goethe, the merest outsiders ; at the best, he was for a time to us an object of intellectual curiosity ; but he has never been a real force in our intellectual life ; and knowledge of his life and thought has at no time been accounted with us more than a luxury for the literary student or the philosopher.

In the following pages I have set before myself the task of reviewing once more Goethe's life and activity in a frankly English way ; of revising the estimates of the man and his work which are, more or less, traditional amongst us ; of presenting the facts in the new light which the labours of German scholars have brought to bear on them ; and, above all, of bringing into prominence these aspects of the poet's work and teaching which have still significance for us at the beginning of the twentieth century.

Beyond the more obvious sources to which every writer on Goethe is indebted, I would especially mention here Prof. Christoph Schrempf's *Goethes Lebensanschauung in ihrer geschichtlichen Entwicklung*, Stuttgart, 1905-7, one of the most suggestive of recent books on Goethe ; and that indispensable summary of Goethe's ripest thought, Prof. Otto Harnack's *Goethe in der Epoche seiner Vollendung*, of which a second edition appeared in 1901.

J. G. ROBERTSON.

LONDON, *April* 1912.

CONTENTS

GOETHE AND THE
TWENTIETH CENTURY

CHAPTER I

GOETHE'S EARLY YEARS

GOETHE'S youth possesses a certain typical significance ; it is not merely a particular poet's beginnings,
but the ideal youth of a poet, a romance into which
would seem to have been woven the most auspicious
elements in the lives of all great poets. It is,
moreover, the supremely interesting part of Goethe's
life, a fact, due to no small extent to its being enshrined for us in one of the most delightful auto-
biographies of the world's literature.

A recent German writer has defined genius as a
combination of three equally essential components :
passion, imaginative alertness and judgment ; and
these qualities are usually present in complementary
proportions in the parents of the man of genius.
In Goethe's case there can be no doubt that the
rarest and most precious part of his genius came
from his mother, his mental sprightliness and his
agile, passionate imagination. But Goethe's mother

A

had character as well ; her personality was strong enough to have left a mark on her age, even had she not been the mother of its greatest poet, and her delightful letters—quite the most delightful letters ever written by a poet's mother—give her a place among the brilliant women that grace so unobtrusively German literature in its classic age. Frau Rat Goethe had the priceless advantage not only of being, as she said, young with her son—she was only seventeen when he was born—but in growing up with him as well, and until her death in 1808, she remained in sympathetic touch with his thought and work.

From Goethe's father came " des Lebens ernste Führung," the energy and the staying power which enabled the young poet to preserve his balance in the many storms to which his sensitive, emotional temperament exposed him. It was just these solid, not to say stolid, qualities he inherited from his father, which prevented him from himself becoming a Werther, a Weisslingen, or a Tasso—men into whose souls he saw with preternatural clearness. But from his father came, too, the somewhat pompous, oracular manner, which grew on Goethe with the years, and occasionally exposed him, as the Weimar Geheimrat, to irreverent gibes on the part of the younger generation.

The poet has himself opened his autobiography

by assuring us that when he came into the world
at Frankfort on the Main on the 28th of August, 1749,
the stars were auspicious. As far as the material
side of life was concerned and the opportunities
for the education of mind and soul, Goethe was a
child of fortune ; he was born, if not in the lap of
luxury, at least amidst substantial, middle-class com-
forts. His father, a jurist of independent means,
counted among the patricians of the Free City, and
his mother was the daughter of the chief magistrate.
The main disadvantage of the poet's fate was that
it brought him into the German world before that
world was quite ready for him. One cannot help
reflecting that, had Goethe been born some ten
years later, he might have stood a whole generation nearer to us to-day. His most impressionable
years of youth would have been passed in a *milieu*
more stimulating than that of Leipzig between 1765
and 1768 ; and the whole balance of his life have been
tilted in favour of the nineteenth rather than the
eighteenth century. He would have been able
to face the problems of the French Revolution as a
younger man, and with less set opinions ; he might
have adapted himself more readily to the conditions
of the Romantic era in which the last three decades
of his life were passed. But such speculations are
necessarily fruitless ; we must look rather to the
many compensations his period brought him ;

and it was surely worth some measure of posthumous
fame, to have been not merely young in the " Sturm
und Drang," but also the leader of that most virile
literary movement of the eighteenth century.

The picturesque vignettes of Goethe's early life
in Frankfort, which in his *Dichtung und Wahrheit*,
he has himself drawn for us with the delicate pen
of a Chodowiecki in words, have been so often
reproduced by Goethe's biographers that they may
be passed over lightly here. Goethe selected the
episodes which he dwells on, with instinctive tact,
with a sense of relevancy to his future development ;
each little trait or incident, however trivial it may
seem, is introduced with a purpose, is a foreshadow-
ing of things that were to come. The marionette-
theatre which Goethe's grandmother gave the
children one Christmas, awakened the boy's dramatic
instincts, and these were further developed by his
visits to the French comedy a little later ; the
episode of the quartering of the art-loving French-
man, Count Thoranc, on the Goethe family,
awakened in the young poet an interest in art ;
the sombre pictures of civil war and foreign invasion,
contrasted with the brilliant pageantry of an imperial coronation in the Frankfort " Römer,"
kindled wider historical and political interests in
his mind ; and his first passion, that for the Frankfort
Gretchen, which all but brought him into serious

conflict with the civil powers, stirred for the first
time, his emotional nature. The ultimate impression which these early chapters of *Dichtung und
Wahrheit* leave on us is one of sunniness ; the same
brilliant sun that lit up in Goethe's memory the
gilded weathercock on the Sachsenhausen bridge,
floods all these scenes. The shadows and the rainy
days were forgotten in the brightening perspective
of a fifty years' vista ; but one can imagine that
Goethe's own buoyant temperament was not likely,
in those early days, to have been much perturbed
by the darker side of the picture.

In 1765, at the age of seventeen, Goethe was sent
by his father to the University of Leipzig to be
trained into a jurist like himself. And here, although
still far from a real awakening of his genius, the
young poet at least came into touch with the literary
movement of the day, such as it was. It can
hardly be said that Goethe's poetic genius was
precocious ; what has been preserved of his early
poetry—he destroyed, it is true, most of it himself—
does not seem a very promising beginning for so
great a poet. Like all the German writers of the
classic age, great as well as small, Goethe responded
with alacrity to every influence to which he happened
to be exposed. In his Leipzig student-days he
diligently imitated the Leipzig poets : he wrote
comedies in alexandrines, of which it is but small

praise to say that they were as good as, or even superior to, their models ; and he composed lyrics inspired by his Leipzig " Mädgen," Käthchen, or, as he called her, Annette Schönkopf, which rarely rise above the anacreontic verse of the gallant " Klein Paris." It is of such things we must think, when we say that Goethe was born before his time ; we have to regret that so great a genius had to learn the rudiments of his art in so barren a school.

The real poet of Goethe's early student-days is to be looked for, not in his verse, but in his letters. In these we find the quick sensitiveness to impression, the intense fullness of life, the passionate unrest, which gave such enormous impelling force to his life. In the vivacious correspondence with his friend Behring, rather than in the jingles to Annette, we detect the man of genius that was to be. The imitative alexandrines of the comedies, *Die Laune des Verliebten* and *Die Mitschuldigen* do little more than give us a glimpse into the distraught state of the young poet's life, and help us to realise on how false a basis he had tried to build it up. But the highs and lows of the artistic temperament are in his letters ; the bewildering alternation of jubila- tion and despondency, which, in 1768, when he was struck down by serious illness, was to give place to unrelieved brooding and despair. Once at home again in Frankfort, his slow convalescence made an inactive life imperative ; he had time to look regretfully back on Leipzig ; and his chief communion was with books. Rousseau became a favourite author, and the influence of a friend of the family, Susanna von Klettenberg, who belonged to the Moravian brotherhood, turned his thoughts to religion and mysticism. The mystic philosophers proved an antidote to the anacreontic trivialities of Leipzig, and from mysticism his thoughts wandered to the no less fascinating pseudo-science of alchemy. Amidst these studies and meditations, which were of obvious significance for the genesis of *Faust*, Goethe's outlook on life was gaining rapidly in seriousness ; the months of convalescence at home in Frankfort, were the preparation for greater things.

CHAPTER II

IN " STURM UND DRANG "

GOETHE's real life as a poet began on that day in April 1770, when he rode through the Metzgertor into Strassburg; for it was in Strassburg that Goethe's father had resolved his son should finish his legal training. The months the young poet lived through so intensely in this town, which, in spite of its French veneer, still remained German at heart, have a deeper significance for Goethe's personal development and the literature of his time than any other period of his career.

Here in Alsace, Goethe's buoyant, elastic temperament recovered from the moodiness of the sickbed; the clouds of Moravian pietism and mysticism were rapidly dispersed. And then, by one of those miraculous concatenations, by which, from time to time, the divine purpose in Goethe's life seemed to be made manifest, Herder arrived in Strassburg. At Herder's feet in the little Hôtel du Louvre, in a darkened room to which the elder writer was condemned during the course of an operation on the eye, Goethe imbibed the new faith of which Herder was the apostle; Rousseau became a power of the

8

first order in his life ; his eyes were opened to the greatness of Shakespeare, of Homer, of Ossian and of folksong ; he became suddenly conscious of the beauty of Gothic architecture so magnificently exemplified in the Minster above his head. The movement of "Sturm und Drang," or "Storm and Stress," in German literature was born in these months in Strassburg ; Goethe threw himself heart and soul into it, and from 1773 onwards he was looked up to by all Germany as a pioneer and leader. "Sturm und Drang" might be described as a phase of militant individualism, the emancipation of the eighteenth-century spirit from the fetters of pseudo-classicism. Its literature bore a predominantly individualistic and personal stamp ; the thoughts and feelings of the young poets themselves, intensified and magnified, formed the immediate theme of all they wrote ; character, rather than incident or plot, was their first care ; and the personal note was of infinitely more importance in their eyes than conformity to cosmopolitan opinion. The tendency of the movement was, above all, anti-classic and national. The models of the "Sturm und Drang" literature, however, were for the most part foreign, and these not merely, like Shakespeare and the *Percy Ballads*, Germanic, or like Ossian, believed by these young poets to be Germanic, but even French. Goethe's *Werther* could never have been written had

there been no *Nouvelle Heloïse* ; the dramatic theory
of the time owed more to Diderot and Lemercier than
to any German predecessor ; and it is possible that
Goethe himself in some of his most imaginative
flights—in the fragments of *Mahomet* and *Cäsar*
—had been led thither all unawares at the hand
of one who seemed to the " Stürmer und Dränger "
to be the embodiment of the rationalism they
opposed—Voltaire.

Goethe's whole intellectual nature, his views of
life and literature, underwent a revolution in this
brief period. He who, not very long before, had
been writing artificial comedies in the French style,
became a fervid worshipper of Shakespeare ; he
extolled Erwin von Steinbach, the planner of the
Strassburg Minster, in a panegyric as unrestrained
as if his Leipzig art-master, Adam Oeser, had never
taught him that severely classic form was alone
worthy of his admiration. The seething ferment
of Rousseau's ideas permeated his whole nature :
Rousseau's stamp is on the theses which, in a public
disputation, he defended for his Strassburg degree ;
Rousseau made it possible for him to appreciate
to the full the primitive masterworks of poetry,
the Bible, Homer, Ossian. The process which the
young poet went through in these months intensified
all his faculties, and rendered him extraordinarily
sensitive to impressions. This is to be seen in the

flood of poetry with which he surrounded at once
the figure of the Alsatian pastor's daughter,
Friederike Brion. The lyrics which Goethe wrote
to Friederike, compared with the rococo verses
inspired by Annette in Leipzig, seem to belong to
another age and another clime. Friederike appears
in the glorifying haze of this intense feeling as a
Madonna of the poet's imagination ; and although
in *Dichtung und Wahrheit* the story may be suffused
by a retrospective glamour which was foreign to it,
we have Goethe's own letters to Friederike to
justify the poetry in which he has enshrined his
feelings for her. The love story ended, as it
had to end, unhappily ; Goethe himself realised
that it could not be otherwise, when he seriously
thought of presenting the Alsatian peasant-girl to
his patrician family in Frankfort ; and the lacera-
tion of feeling which the breach with her meant,
initiated the young poet into that "sanctuary
of sorrows" from which the greatest works of this
optimist at heart so often emerged.

Meanwhile Goethe's academic career had reached
its close ; he had obtained the diploma which
entitled him to call himself "doctor," and to practise
as an advocate. He returned to Frankfort bringing
with him the all but finished manuscript of his first
important drama, *Gottfried von Berlichingen mit
der eisernen Hand*. This work did not, however,

appear until 1773, and then, condensed and altered, under the title *Götz von Berlichingen.*

Götz von Berlichingen is the typical drama of the early "Sturm und Drang," as Schiller's *Räuber* is of the later development of that movement. It was not, however, put forward by its author as a drama for the stage, but as a dramatised reproduction of a chronicle ; and it is thus hardly fair to regard it merely as a not very successful attempt to imitate Shakespeare. Goethe rather selected from Shakespeare's work those elements which appealed to him personally and responded to a need of the time. It may have been a strange obliquity of vision which allowed the "Sturm und Drang" only to see one aspect of Shakespeare's art, only his gigantic heroes and villains, and to be oblivious to his architectural construction which had appealed to Lessing's critical mind ; but the European theatre had stagnated too long under the rule of artificial law, to leave room for much sympathy with laws of any kind. *Götz von Berlichingen* is Shakespearean only in so far as it attempts to present a great character by throwing light on that character from every possible side. And in doing so, Goethe took, one might say, unfair advantage of the Shakespearean method of constantly changing place and time ; and he introduced contrasting figures regardless of their economy in the action as a whole. Every-

thing, in fact, was subordinated to the development
and display of the central character. But just this
neglect of other considerations led Goethe into fresh
difficulties ; for as his work proceeded he found
himself more and more attracted by the subjective
possibilities of the subsidiary character of Weisslingen, who soon became the most living and human
personage of the tragedy. It required all the poet's
self-denial to repress, in view of the unity of the
drama, his growing interest in this Weisslingen,
who sinned and suffered as the poet himself had
sinned and suffered in Strassburg. *Götz* makes no
pretence to be a historical drama in the modern
sense of that word ; of those subtler elements that
go to make up the picture of a past time, *milieu*,
atmosphere, archaism of word and thought, there
is little in Goethe's work ; it cannot be judged by the
standards of modern historical realism. But what
we do get in Goethe's tragedy is an extraordinarily
vivid reproduction of the sixteenth-century chronicle,
as it was reflected in Goethe's mind ; we see it
translated, as it were, into terms of Rousseau and
leavened by personal experiences. Goethe's theories
of dramatic form and construction may have been
extravagant aberrations of only passing interest,
but in the great, unconscious art of drawing living
people, Goethe revealed himself in *Götz* as a creative
poet of the first order. It is in this power that

the attraction of the drama still lies for us to-day.

Goethe returned to Frankfort and made a beginning to learning the practical side of his profession. But it was clear that law had less hold on him than ever ; his university training behind him, it virtually ceased to interest him at all. Meanwhile he had gathered round him a circle of sympathetic and admiring friends, in Darmstadt as well as in Frankfort itself. Of these, Johann Heinrich Merck seems to have had the deepest influence on him. Merck had a sharp, ironic tongue and provided, like Mephistopheles to Faust, or Don Carlos to Clavigo, the antidote to that excessive revelling in feeling to which the enthusiastic disciple of Rousseau too readily resigned himself. In all Goethe's friendships antithesis of temperament formed a stronger and closer bond than sympathy : it was as if that desire for harmonious balance, which was so characteristic of him all his life long, influenced even the choice of his intimates. Goethe's literary convictions found expression in the criticisms of the *Frankfurter Gelehrte Anzeigen*, where the irresponsible iconoclasm of his views on books and writers is of less account than his apostrophic asides and monologues in his own person. He was not, however, disposed to take root in his native town, and he welcomed the proposal of his father that he should put the coping-stone to his legal apprenticeship by spending a few months at the Imperial Courts then established in Wetzlar. In May, 1772, he left Frankfort once more.

Wetzlar was no more calculated to stimulate in Goethe an interest in his profession than the lectures at Strassburg or the practical work in Frankfort had been. The business of the courts there stagnated, or was carried on so leisurely and with such inadequate resources that cases had been waiting more than a hundred and fifty years for settlement ; there was little temptation even for a zealous jurist to interest himself in the procedure. But this mattered little to the young poet. Once more, as in Alsace, spring vibrated through his sensitive nature : and, Homer in hand, he let the new impressions meet and mingle in him. Friends he had, of course, in plenty, and they were not limited to the professional men he met daily round the dinner-table of the inn ; wherever he went he was a welcome guest, and at this period of his life he seems to have had in a high degree the art of winning the hearts of children. It would have been surprising if, amidst all these crowding new impressions, love had not again, as in Strassburg, participated. This time his heart was set on fire by the affianced bride of one of the legation secretaries, Kestner, and a good friend of his own. Charlotte

Buff was the eldest daughter of the resident
" Amtmann " or chief magistrate of the town, and
had few qualifications for playing the sentimental
heroine. Distinctly practical, she seems to have
attracted Goethe by her cheerful, social qualities
rather than by any real emotional depth ; she
pleased him best when surrounded by her younger
brothers and sisters, to whom she acted as a mother.
He met her on the occasion of a ball, to which it
had fallen to him to accompany her ; love, as
was always the case with Goethe, was kindled at
first sight, and his imagination did the rest. It
is noticeable what weight Goethe usually ascribes
to his first meeting with the women who played
a rôle in his life ; one cannot help thinking that
they might have played that rôle even had no
closer intimacy followed ; in other words, the emotion was often, in great measure, a product of the
poet's imagination. It is not easy for us nowadays
to form a clear estimate of Goethe's passion for
Lotte ; his actual relations to Lotte and Kestner
are so inextricably blended with the fictitious
presentation of them in *Werthers Leiden*, that it is
impossible to keep them apart. Even in Goethe's
own memory, when he came to write his autobiography, the " Dichtung " was a more conspicuous
factor than the " Wahrheit," and he all unconsciously
ascribed to the real Lotte and his feelings for her,

qualities which were only true of the imagined Lotte of the book ; it was certainly the imagined Lotte, not the real one, that brought her lover to the brink of suicide. Were it not that in after years Goethe spoke of his passion for Charlotte Buff as one of the deepest of his life, we should hardly be justified in regarding it as one of his more serious affairs. Goethe's whole nature was at this time so highly sensitised that even a passing fancy might have been capable of producing a work like *Werther*.

With *Die Leiden des jungen Werther* (1774) Goethe took the world by storm as no German writer before him had done. It is easy to say that the art of *Werther* is truer than that of *Götz von Berlichingen* because it is more photographic ; but such a judgment over-looks the subtle poetic transmutation to which reality is here subjected. In the first place, *Werther* is the artistic product of more than one phase of Goethe's own life. After the passion for Lotte in Wetzlar, from which the poet saved himself, as in Strassburg, by flight, he did not return direct to Frankfort, but paid a visit to Frau von Laroche, the friend of Wieland and one of the chief women of letters of the older generation. Here at Ehren-breitstein, amidst new surroundings, the memories of Lotte were transferred to a new acquaintance, Maximiliane, the daughter of his hostess, soon to become the wife of Peter Brentano an elderly

B

merchant in Frankfort. Some critics of *Werthers Leiden* would distinguish two phases in the novel, an earlier one inspired by Goethe's Wetzlar experiences, a later by his interest in Maximiliane ; they find in the heroine of the novel, a composite picture of two women, or rather, a portrait of Lotte Buff merging imperceptibly into one of Maximiliane Laroche, an Albert made up partly of Kestner, partly of Maximiliane's later husband, a Werther partly the poet himself, partly the young jurist, whose death by his own hand first suggested the form of the novel to Goethe. But there is no outward trace of inartistic dualism in the characters of the novel ; they are welded so skilfully that only a superrefinement of criticism is able to draw such fine distinctions. It would rather appear that in all external features Wetzlar and Goethe's life there provided the facts, while the subjective elements, the spiritual experiencings which give vitality to the book, were the more immediate impressions of Ehrenbreitstein. The heroine is, in other words, at heart more Maximiliane than Lotte ; Albert more Maximiliane's husband than Kestner, while Werther is a fusion of two Goethes, a reflex of Goethe himself in two quite different situations. If *Werther* is a truer, more sincere creation than *Götz*, it is not because it is more of a photograph, but because it is built up on a truer intuition. In spite of the

stumbling-block which the rather musty senti-
mentality of *Werther* puts in the way of the modern
reader, it will always remain, by virtue of its sincerity
and truth, one of the vital novels of the eighteenth
century.

With these two works Goethe put himself in the
front rank of German writers ; and life began to
assume a new aspect to him. He was eagerly sought
out by new admirers, such as Lavater, Basedow,
and the two brothers Jacobi; and from all he
received quite as much as he gave. Lavater had,
by infusing something of the sturdy individualistic
spirit of the " Sturm und Drang " into the religion
of the day, raised it, in Goethe's eyes, above the
dull level of pietism and freed it from the depressing
influence of Lutheran orthodoxy ; while from the
younger Jacobi he learned to recognise in Spinoza
the philosopher whose thought was most in harmony
with his own.

Contrary to the expectations of his friends—
and the mere disappointment of such expectations
was perhaps the best sign of the healthy, growing
state of Goethe's genius—he had not followed up
Götz and *Werther* with works at all similar. The
novel he gave up altogether ; and in the field of the
drama he turned in the first instance to more modern
and domestic themes. *Clavigo* was a play of Goethe's
own time, indeed, so much of his own time, that the

hero, a Spaniard mentioned in the *Mémoires* of Beaumarchais, was still alive, and heard with amusement that he was being killed nightly on German stages ! *Clavigo* bulked less largely in the eyes of the world than its predecessor ; but as a drama it is less open to adverse criticism than *Götz*. The restlessness of the Shakespearean technique has given place, under the influence of Lessing and Diderot, to a soberer sequence of scenes and events, which was better adapted to the eighteenth-century stage. In fineness of character-drawing the advance is even greater ; instead of the broad, vague lines, which too often obscure the picture in the first drama, we have here miniature-like portraits ; in other words, in passing from *Götz* to *Clavigo* Goethe went through the same development towards realistic truth which is to be seen in the transition from *Götz* to *Werther*. One has but to compare Clavigo with Weisslingen, or the two Maries with each other, to turn, above all, to the magnificent figure of Don Carlos, the subtlest that Goethe had yet drawn, to realise the advance. The dialogue between Clavigo and Don Carlos—especially in the fourth act—belongs to the most poignantly modern that the dramatic literature of the eighteenth century has to show.

Stella, ein Schauspiel für Liebende, is also, like *Clavigo*, a " modern " tragedy, and it awakened an unfair amount of contempt, abhorrence and ridicule, to which we in England, with our *Rovers*, contributed our share. But, quite apart from the fact that to the student of Goethe's personality in these years, this play—hardly excepting *Werther*, his most subjective "Sturm und Drang" work—has a quite peculiar interest, it deserves more serious consideration than it usually receives. It is at every point inferior in form to its predecessor, but in intention it is again a step forward in the direction of that finer psychological art of which Goethe proved himself in later years so skilful a master; *Stella* is, in this respect, a direct predecessor of *Tasso*. But it was, unfortunately, a mere hasty sketch, a drama born of the innate need of giving voice to his own difficulties and troubles; the poet allowed himself no time to reflect on his subject, and the conciliatory close which leaves the hero with two wives—however interesting it may be as an expression of advanced "Sturm und Drang" ideas —was too little in consonance with civilised conventions, to stand; Goethe himself realised how unsatisfactory his play was, and cut the knot by providing a new ending which converted it into a tragedy.

The lighter side of Goethe's temperament in these years, found expression in dramatic satires, in which he let his wit play alike round the fogies of tradition, and the too advanced pioneers of the new gospel of individual freedom ; and the " Singspiel," or vaudeville, provided an outlet for the lyric as well as the dramatic side of his genius. But more significant than any of these trifles were the various fragments of this period. Nowhere is the extraordinary richness of Goethe's inspiration more apparent than in the variety of the themes which he singled out for poetic treatment. He planned great tragedies on Socrates and Mahomet ; an epic on the Wandering Jew ; to 1773 belongs the noble fragment of a drama on *Prometheus* ; and, most marvellous of all, *Faust* was written in its earliest form, in these Frankfort years. The discovery, in 1885, of a manuscript copy of this " *Urfaust* " put an end to the speculations in which scholars had previously indulged as to the oldest form of Goethe's greatest poem. The Frankfort *Faust* virtually contains all the purely human elements of the tragedy ; the final polish is alone wanting ; and one cannot help thinking that the later additions have sometimes destroyed the freshness and simplicity of the original conception. Besides *Faust*, Goethe took with him to Weimar in a forward state of composition his drama of *Egmont*, and possibly also a sketch of what was ultimately to become *Wilhelm Meisters Lehrjahre*.

At the very beginning of the year 1775 there was

kindled in Goethe's inflammable heart a new love,
this time for a type of woman of whom hitherto
he had had little experience. At first sight,
it might have seemed hardly likely that Lili
Schönemann, the daughter of a Frankfort banker,
who moved in the gay social circles of the
Frankfort plutocracy and had necessarily none of
Goethe's interests, could have attracted him, or,
having attracted him, have held him. Indeed,
Goethe was conscious from the first of the disparity
of the two worlds to which Lili and he belonged.
Her circle was uncongenial to him, often repugnant ;
he felt instinctively that to be bound up too closely
with it, would inevitably mean an estrangement
from the real work of his life. Her attractions,
however, proved too strong, and events took the
only course which they could take under the circumstances : Goethe became formally betrothed.
The moment, however, that he felt himself bound,
he began to realise the value of his previous
freedom. A favourable opportunity for reviewing
the whole situation objectively and dispassionately
offered itself in an invitation from the two brothers
Stolberg to accompany them to Switzerland ; and he
accepted, hoping that the distractions of this journey
might help him to face the world without Lili.
He did not come as satisfactorily out of the experiment as he had hoped ; Lili was not so easily erased

from his memory. But the conviction was at least strengthened in him that to bind himself irrevocably to her would be folly ; and, in the end, the engagement was by mutual consent broken off. The Swiss tour was extended as far as the top of the St Gotthard Pass, from which Goethe cast longing eyes down into Italy, the land of promise, which had had such magic attraction for him since his childhood.

Again the kindly fates that seemed to lead Goethe by the hand, interposed. The young Duke of Saxe-Weimar, Karl August, arrived in Frankfort, on his way to bring home his bride from Darmstadt, and invited Goethe to accompany him to Weimar on his return journey. Goethe held himself in readiness to accept the invitation. It looked, however, as if, at the last moment, a hitch had occurred ; for the messenger with the final summons did not arrive. Meanwhile Goethe felt that, whatever happened, he could not remain in Frankfort ; the break must be made quickly—if not Weimar, then Italy ; and he had actually set out on his southward journey, when the Duke's courier overtook him.

Schiller in his familiar classification of the poets, placed Goethe among the " naïve " writers ; but he did not take count of the fact that there was not one Goethe but a series of Goethes all differing from one another just in respect of this quality of naïveté.

The Goethe of these fertile Frankfort years was most naïve of all ; he allowed no "sentimental" or reflective element to creep in between himself and his creative work. In those days poetry was for him, not merely a direct "confession," but a necessity. This explains the unique charm of this period to the modern reader ; it is the reason why so many writers have preferred to study and discuss the "young Goethe" in preference to the riper, wiser Goethe of after years. The works he threw out then with such prodigality mean comparatively little to us to-day : but they are the best products of an age, the striving of which was to be fundamental, to get at the heart of things, to be done with untrue conventions and shams. To feel, to think, to act, in perfect harmony and with absolute singleness of purpose ; to attune one's whole personality to nature ; to be one with her—that was the ideal behind the "Sturm und Drang" ; and it was Goethe's. Above all, to feel—all else was subsidiary. This disproportionate significance attached to the emotional, compared with the intellectual nature perhaps explains why Goethe, who in later years, attached such weight to the proper balance between the two, was in these years so exclusively a love-poet. His eroticism appears here against a purple background of renunciation and resignation ; but the conflicts are, as yet, on the surface ; they

have not the subtlety and depth of his later search-
ing of the heart.   The supreme crime to the young
Goethe was the crime which lay heaviest on his
own conscience, that of lack of emotional constancy ;
and it is the motive force which lies behind the
tragedies of these years.

CHAPTER III

GOETHE IN WEIMAR TO 1786

EARLY on the morning of November 7th, 1775, before daybreak, Goethe arrived in Weimar. The break with Frankfort, with Lili, with the old ways of feeling and thinking, the old friends, has been made. An entirely new chapter began in his life. There is probably a good deal of idle gossip and exaggeration in the accounts of the " merry time " which followed Goethe's arrival ; but there was not much room for seriousness of any kind in a small German " Residenz " under the old *régime* of the eighteenth century. The spirit of dilettantism made itself felt everywhere : dilettantism was the prevailing note in the fatherly, personal interest which the court and governing classes took in the welfare of the people ; there was and could be no higher, serious political thought or action, no reason to hold strong party-views on any question at all. Consequently literature, art, social amusements, played a large part in the life of the town ; and the universal attitude to all these things was that of the unserious, amusement-seeking amateur.

The young poet took on the colour of his surroundings ; he who, for a few years, had been looked up to in Frankfort as a leader of men, became an amateur among amateurs ; he, who had been the creator of elemental figures like Götz, Werther, Faust, Prometheus, found his occupation gone in the trivial atmosphere of this court ; a short time before bursting with creative energy, he lapsed now into a state of complete quiescence. In the fullness of time no one could be more merciless than Goethe in castigating dilettantism, but for some months at least, he was given over to it body and soul. He composed " Singspiele " for courtly amateurs to act ; he wrote a novel about a young man who becomes an amateur of the theatre ; and even the noble work with which a new epoch in his creative work begins, *Iphigenie auf Tauris*, was originally a *pièce d'occasion* written for and performed by amateurs, himself among the number.

The note on which *Dichtung und Wahrheit* closes, the famous words from *Egmont* : " As if lashed by invisible spirits, the sun-horses of time dash off with the light chariot of our destiny, and nothing remains for us but, with brave hearts, to hold fast to the reins and guide the wheels, to the right, to the left, from a stone here, a precipice there," was a constantly recurring one in Goethe's life, as indeed it could hardly fail to be with one whose career was so steadily favoured by fortune. Probably Goethe himself would have regarded the turn events now took, freeing him from the restrictions of his Frankfort life, the disturbing passion for Lili and the intolerable paternal rule, as a manifestation of the good-will of the Higher Powers. But when one sees this young man of twenty-six, who had the world at his feet, who, in the brief space of four years, had shown such unexampled creative energy and given voice to such world-compelling thoughts, sinking into the amateur, one is inclined to question if Goethe's fate was a kindly one after all.

For a time there was, no doubt, a very real danger that Goethe would succumb to the temptations of this easy-going dilettantism. He had, however, an extraordinary power of righting himself; he was always able to rise superior to his surroundings ; and before very long we find him beginning to rebel against conditions, to the pettiness of which he gave expression in *Tasso*, and which, in later life, in the Second Part of *Faust*, he caricatured. As soon as Goethe realised how little the ties that bound him in the first instance to Weimar, really meant to him, he might conceivably have turned his back upon the court and returned to that freedom which he had regarded as so desirable when he fled to Switzerland from the hemming conventions of a possible union with Lili Schönemann ; and this was the more likely as the differences with his father began to assume a serious form, the latter refusing to send his son money. But the court influence had given place to other ties, which made a break with Weimar less easy. To the first place among these belongs his love for Charlotte von Stein, to the second Herder's acceptance of an invitation to make Weimar his home.

It is interesting to observe how the various women Goethe loved seem in turn to harmonise with the surroundings in which he happened to be placed at the time; they appear as poetic geniuses of place. Thus Käthchen Schönkopf is the embodiment of the Saxon rococo; the mood of Goethe's Strassburg life is concentrated in Friederike; that of Wetzlar in Lotte, of Frankfort in Lili; and now Weimar is reflected in Frau von Stein. Frau von Stein is usually described as the noblest woman whom Goethe ever loved, the most worthy of his love. And this is no doubt true. There has been much unnecessary writing to prove that this love of Goethe for a woman of mature years, the mother of seven children was more of the nature of an intellectual friendship; but the distinguishing feature was rather that the love for Frau von Stein began in friendship and respect, and that it made greater claims on Goethe's intellectual nature than his other loves had done. For the rest, one can follow distinctly through those wonderful love-letters of

Goethe's to her—her letters to Goethe were almost all destroyed — the various phases, the warm, respectful friendship deepening into passion, until the moment comes when it threatens to close over Goethe's head and he is obliged to save himself by flight ; the unhappy struggle against obsession then gradually gives place to a calmer objectivity, similar to the objectivity that brought tranquillity into his relations with Lili ; and the end comes with the substitution of new ties.

It was obviously no mere platonic friendship that inspired the beautiful lyric poetry of this period of Goethe's life. Poems like *Wonne der Wehmut* or *An den Mond* may not be directly inspired love-poems, such as we owe to Friederike or Lili ; but in these Weimar years a change had came over Goethe's whole attitude to the poetic expression of personal emotion ; the purely subjective note has disappeared from his lyrics as from his dramas and his prose. The feeling that lies behind the poetry of this time is as deep and sincere as ever, but it is tempered by the growing objectivity of the classic artist in Goethe.

In no period of Goethe's life do we miss the steady documentary evidence of growth and achievement so much as here ; his letters do not throw the right kind of light on his work for our purpose ; his diaries are inadequate.   We are consequently thrown back to a great extent on inference, in tracing the remarkable change that came over Goethe from the moment when he arrived in Weimar, with the yeast of " Sturm und Drang " still fermenting in his veins, to the period when he made good his escape to Italy in 1786. The actual literature he has left us from this period is restricted to a few beautiful lyrics and ballads, two or three " Singspiele," a charming little one-act comedy, *Die Geschwister*, and a record of a visit to the Harz Mountains. Besides these, it is true, we have *Iphigenie auf Tauris* in its earliest form and a first sketch of his novel, then called *Wilhelm Meisters theatralische Sendung*, of which a copy was recently discovered in Zürich ; and we can infer with some degree of accuracy what was done to *Egmont* and *Tasso* in these years. But a record of this fragmentary nature is necessarily unsatisfactory and inadequate to establish even the most fundamental dates in the poet's development, such as, for instance, when exactly the " Sturm und Drang " in Goethe's life gave place to a soberer, calmer outlook.

We cannot but feel some disappointment in the literary leanness of the early years in Weimar, following, as they did, upon a period of such activity. It has been argued that, in this period, Goethe was deepening his spiritual life, enriching his experience, undergoing, in contact with men and the affairs of state, an educational process which was to leave its mark on his later work.   The young Duke of Weimar, influenced by Frederick the Great's flattering patronage of Voltaire, gave Goethe a responsible share in the conduct of state affairs, and that in opposition to his advisers, who naturally and with justice thought that Goethe's precedents, his literary activity, his inexperience of routine, were not recommendations.   And it is greatly to the credit of the Duke's judgment and a tribute to Goethe's many-sided genius and stability of character that the trust imposed upon him was not misplaced. Under the patriarchal conditions reigning in the Duchy of Weimar, Goethe was an exemplary minister of State.   He took an active interest in affairs, showed excellent practical judgment in dealing with people, and his want of bureaucratic routine had, at least, the advantage of preventing him becoming the slave of it.

Moreover, this wider activity was quite in accordance with Goethe's own views ; at no time of his career did he regard himself as a man of letters pure and simple ; often, indeed, he imagined his chief strength lay in quite other fields.   His constant aim was to live as full and complete a life as possible ; the writing of books was merely a concomitant accident.   His ideal is nowhere more finely expressed than in his often quoted simile

C

of the pyramid : " The daily work, which has been meted out to me, which becomes every day easier and harder to me, demands my presence, awake or dreaming. This duty becomes continually dearer to me, and in fulfilling it, I wish to be the equal of the greatest men, and in nothing greater. This desire to raise the apex of the pyramid of my existence, the basis of which has been given and laid for me, as high as possibly into the air, surpasses all else, and can hardly for a moment be forgotten. I must lose no time, I am already on in years and fate may perhaps break me in the middle and the Babylon-tower be left blunt and uncompleted. At least it shall be said : it was boldly planned ; and if I live, my powers, with God's favour, will hold out until I reach the top." This was written in September, 1780.

This conception of human endeavour and activity was inherently bound up with eighteenth-century humanism ; fullness, totality, was an essential element in the educational schemes of that dominantly pedagogic age ; any kind of specialisation or narrowing down of the activities of the individual life was abhorrent to the Rousseaus, Basedows, Pestalozzis and the authors of the various " Fürstenspiegel " in which the best ideals were mapped out for the benefit of future rulers of absolute monarchies. At bottom, this striving after universality of culture was only a development, on more humane lines, of the intellectual aspirations of the " Polyhistor " of an earlier generation. And just as there was a very obvious dark side to the polyhistoric ideals, so this later phase of universalism was not without its serious disadvantages. One cannot help thinking that Goethe the artist suffered at the hands of Goethe the philosopher, the statesman, the scientist. We are ready to recognise that the perfect artist is the rarest type of genius, and we know that Goethe had in him, all that goes to making the supreme artist in letters. We consequently resent the time occupied in taking over the duties of a minister of State, in studying drawing and painting, with a zeal that was not justified by the actual results, or even in controverting Newton, and forestalling Darwin. All these activities which might have been admirable in a lesser man, appear, to say the least of it, unfortunate in the greatest poetic genius of the eighteenth century.

It has been argued that Goethe's greatness in his own peculiar province benefited by these incursions into other fields, that his mind was broadened, his sympathies universalised. But looking frankly at the actual facts, we are obliged to admit that the contribution of such experiences to Goethe's poetic achievement was out of proportion to the energy he devoted to acquiring them. The great art-work of the world is, as Goethe himself well knew, conceived " im Dunkeln," or to use Schiller's expression, is " naïve," instinctive. Being a minister of State does not help a writer very far when he has to recreate in poetry the momentous events of history ; on the other hand, it is usually just the common happenings and the common experiences of life that are best adapted to be transmuted by the poet into the pure gold of those unique and typical experiences which make great art. It may be frankly questioned if the universality of Goethe's interests and experiences added one inch to his stature as a poet ; rather one might say that it was responsible for that interruption of his interest which led to long delays in the composition of individual works, to fragmentary incompleteness in not a few, and in still others, to an overweening deference to æsthetic theories and abstract considerations.

As the years moved on in Weimar, Goethe felt less and less satisfied with the primrose path into which his fate had led him. The bonds of amateurism became burdensome to him ; and in his saner moments he may even have recognised that his statesmanship was, after all, only amateurism on a larger scale ; that his boasted wideness of interests in art and science was but a frittering away of time, which in no wise contributed to the building and strengthening

of the pyramid of his existence. He was a good
enough judge of his own achievement to realise
that the *Iphigenie* he had first written for the amusement of his amateur world, was too big a creation
for such a world and that his own unique powers
ought not to be squandered in ministering to an
amusement-seeking court. Slowly, too, the truth
was perhaps dawning on him that it is " in limitation that the master first shows himself," or that
deeper conviction which came to him with increasing
force as the years moved on : " I have really been
born for an æsthetic activity." Here perhaps lay a
truer reason for the feverish flight to Italy in 1786
than in the mere endeavour to get rid of the outward
ties that bound and galled him in Weimar.

CHAPTER IV

IN ITALY ; " EGMONT," " IPHIGENIE," " TASSO," " MEISTER "

THE yearning for Italy runs through the German imagination of the eighteenth century, like a silver thread ; it provided a never-failing strain of romanticism even in periods of the most forbidding classic taste. In Goethe's case one might say that it was an inheritance from father to son, a longing first awakened in early childhood in the old Frankfort house with its Italian books and its pictures of Italy ; and he had been on the way to Italy, it will be remembered, when the final invitation to Weimar reached him in 1775. Italy, however, was too constant an element in the German literary mind for this to be a matter of accident. One might trace the love of the Germanic north for the south— the longing of the fir for the pine, as Hans Christian Andersen called it—back to the days when the Renaissance first cast its spell ; to the sober, uninspired seventeenth century, when Germany lay hidebound under the classicism of the Renaissance. Then it was that the Marinistic writers of Italy pointed out the way to freedom from the

classic yoke, even although that way was a devious
and questionable one. All through the eighteenth
century, again, Italy, as the home of the antique,
was the goal to which men like Winkelmann and
Lessing looked, who sought in ancient Greek art a
purification from the grosser elements of pseudo-
classic taste.

To Goethe the visit to Italy was an event of
magnitude—the central event of his life. We
see this in the long spiritual preparation that
preceded it; in his feverish anxiety at the last lest
some unforeseen obstacle should thwart his plan,
once it was conceived; in the haste with which the
poet fled across the Brenner, and in his unwillingness to return to Germany. Possibly the attraction
of Italy was not alone responsible for all this.
The desire to flee the entanglements of Weimar
life, its narrowness and provincialism, its dilettantism; to break the tightening bonds of his
relationship with Charlotte von Stein—these things,
no doubt, had their share. But, once there, the
delight of Goethe with Italy was unfeigned, un-
bounded. Every page of the *Italienische Reise*
bears witness to it; he became for the time, an
Italian among Italians, or, at least, a Roman among
Romans. Rome was the first large city Goethe
had ever seen; and the whole weight of humanistic
traditions, education and taste combined to endear

it to him, to make it appear what it still was in the eighteenth century, the veritable capital of the world. Not since the Frankfort days of "Sturm und Drang" had Goethe lived so intensely as he now lived in Rome, in the company of German artists and of the silent monuments of antiquity.

It has been said of Goethe's Italian journey that the most interesting thing about it was not what the poet saw, but what he did not see. He went to Italy pre-eminently on the quest of the antique ; the great Renaissance sculptors and painters only attracted him in so far as he found in them a reflection of the glory of a still remoter past. Only for Palladio in Verona and Padua, for Michael Angelo in Rome did he feel something of that enthusiasm with which the ancient treasures of the Vatican and the ruins of the Eternal City filled him. But the Romantic Italy of the Renaissance he hardly saw at all ; he visited Venice without being moved by the gorgeous canvasses of Paolo Veronese or Tintoretto ; Florence meant little to him ; Giotto and Botticelli he never mentions ; Raphael alone receives a reasonable share of appreciation. In fact, it was as the disciple of Winkelmann that Goethe visited Rome, as the heir of a purely classic tradition.

Goethe had gone to Italy not merely to see ; he sought a new philosophy and a new æsthetics. The old "Sturm und Drang" individualism had

had its day with him ; he looked back on it with
repugnance. Like all the great minds of the eighteenth century, he had the innate craving for law
and order from which his youthful " Sturm und
Drang "—at least so it now seemed to him—had
been but a wanton aberration ; he sought again
the shelter of the classic fold, and the ideal of art
he found in Italy was but a reversion to the old
Renaissance ideal, purified, ennobled and brought
into line with the humanistic strivings of his age.

The supreme importance of the Italian Journey
for Goethe's own personal life and development
lay in the fact that he was able here for the first
time to view himself objectively, to regard his
achievement and ambition from a point of vantage.
He busied himself, all his life long, with himself ;
but rarely did he see himself so clearly and de-
tached as now. In the midst of this new, strange
milieu, he could look back dispassionately on all
he had attained, and make plans for the future.
One night in Rome, Goethe had a dream in which
he saw himself sitting alone in a vessel ; this vessel
was being laden by an invisible hand with splendid
pheasants, whose brilliant plumage glittered in the
sunshine. These pheasants, so he interpreted his
dream, are the rich impressions my life here has given
me ; and with this vessel I will return to Germany
and unload its treasures before my countrymen.

But just in the unloading of his vessel Goethe was
to meet with one of the most disheartening rebuffs
of his life ; for his countrymen would have none of
his pheasants. He left Italy in 1788 with an intensity of regret, which shows how much he had been
at home there ; he returned to Germany a stranger.
He did not reckon with the fact that Germany had
in these months not grown with him ; he found
Weimar where he had left it ; found the German
public still delighting in " Sturm und Drang "
productions like Heinse's *Ardinghello* and Schiller's
Räuber, productions from which, in his newly-
awakened classic ardour, he turned away in disgust.
The consequence was that he retired within himself,
disheartened and embittered. The passion for Charlotte von Stein had gradually burned itself out in
Italy, where lighter loves weakened his memories of
her ; and on his return to Weimar he found solace
in a new companion, Christiane Vulpius, who at
least made no demands on him comparable with
the obsession of his pre-Italian days. In this new
tie an unexpected change made itself felt ; by
degrees Goethe found the quiet domesticity which
Christiane was able to offer him, indispensable to his
well-being ; and it proved a more solid bedrock of
happiness than romantic passion or even intellectual
sympathy. Where so little was asked for, the disturbing element of change was eliminated, and

Christiane, unworthy as she may have been to be his companion, became the helpmate of his life. His marriage with her was not, however, solemnised until later, and years had to pass before her companionship really influenced Goethe's life beneficially. The period which immediately followed his visit to Italy was an unhappy one; he was more completely out 'of tune with his world than he had perhaps ever been before. He turned away from poetry, and buried himself in scientific studies; and these afforded a surer refuge from the distractions of his psychic and emotional life, than that confessional of poetry in which, in earlier days, he had found a panacea for all ills.

Thus the importance of the Italian Journey for Goethe's life can hardly be overestimated; it was perhaps the very greatest event in his whole range of experience. This is abundantly evident from the works which owed their completion to Italy; and these—above all, *Egmont*, *Iphigenie*, *Tasso*, and in a lesser degree, associated with Italy, *Meister* and *Faust*—remain his most vital creations, the creations that have best stood the test of time. In comparing them with the writings of his " Sturm und Drang " period, or still better, with the " Sturm und Drang " form in which three of them were originally conceived, we are conscious of a complete change in the poet's standpoint to his work.

Goethe has now abandoned or lost that phenomenal spontaneity which compelled our admiration in *Götz*, *Clavigo* and *Werther*. His work has ceased to be the realistic presentation of things seen and experienced, in which the pure imitative instinct alone guides his pen; it has now been invaded by æsthetic principles of composition; it has become a mediate, self-conscious art.

Egmont is obviously the work which first claims our attention; for it is, in all essentials, a product of Goethe's " Sturm und Drang." What was added at a later date, although significant for Goethe's development, does not add to or detract materially from our estimate of the play as it was conceived in Frankfort. The labours of modern scholars have, moreover, defined pretty accurately the growth of the play, in separating out the elements added in Weimar and Italy from the original Frankfort matrix. But with this, we need hardly concern ourselves. The charm of the drama, which is due almost exclusively to the personality of its hero, has nothing to do with those widening political and artistic ideas which left their traces on the last revision. Of all Goethe's dramatic works, *Egmont* has perhaps the least claim to the designation of drama; from the point of view of construction it is defective in the extreme; it sins against the established tenets of dramatic *technique*; and it has hardly even a plot. But just in these very defects we see how necessary caution is in judging the vagaries of a creative artist ; for *Egmont* is no failure, and there have been critics, like the French romanticist Ampère, who have placed it at the very head of all Goethe's dramatic writings. In fact, *Egmont* atones for its lack of construction by a quality which is infinitely rarer in poetry, that instinctive power of visualising, of placing living men and women before us, of which Goethe had given a foretaste in his earlier " Sturm und Drang " plays. Graf Egmont and Klärchen, are still amongst the most delightful figures of the European theatre ; for Goethe has succeeded in conveying to us that magnetic quality in their per- sonalities, which they manifest in their relations to each other. These characters alone outweigh the tendency to theatrical convention in Alba, or the unreal opera-like close of the whole, a close which shows how difficult it was for Goethe to see the world he peopled from the point of view of tragedy.

It is with *Iphigenie*, however, that we emerge into the clearer, serener atmosphere of Italy. The drama, as has been already indicated, owed its origin to the early years of Goethe's life in Weimar ; but it passed through several phases, was turned from verse into prose, and from prose back again

into verse. And through these various stages we
see the ultimate masterpiece emerging from a form
not very different from that of the pseudo-classic
plays of the eighteenth century, French and German.
The perfecting of Goethe's *Iphigenie* is a testimony
to the value of externals in poetry ; for the matter
of the drama changed but little from first to last ;
and yet how vast is the difference ! Obviously
Goethe approached literature here from a quite
other standpoint than in the days of *Götz* and
Werther : then " nature " was his ideal ; now
" nature " matters little or not at all. The goal has
become concentrated poetic thought, perfection of
form and execution. And we have to admit that
in this case, exquisiteness of form more than makes
up for the lack of the spontaneous realism in the
creations of Goethe's youth. On *Iphigenie* there
lies a peculiar consecration : every thought, every
word, every gesture is attuned in harmony ; here
is style in a sense not common to the literatures of
the north, style as we know it in the masterworks
of Greece and Italy, of France and Spain. The
glamour of this poetry throws a spell over the
modern reader as of a Greek temple ; before such
pregnant, melodious verses, such calm evenness of
execution, criticism, for a time at least, is dumb.

But when we look more carefully into the poem,
we see that it is not built on so sure a founda-

tion of poetic truth as we may at first have been inclined to believe. To begin with, we are tempted to ask what could have induced Goethe to revive this, surely by no means the most modern or adaptable of the old Greek drama-sagas ? It was not Goethe's way to approach any work in the manner of a literary artisan ; he wrote nothing that was not prompted in the first instance by some experience of his own. Now, the point of subjective sympathy in the story of Iphigenia was clearly the psychic problem of Orestes' fate. Goethe had himself been an Orestes ; he had fled from Friederike, from Lili, and was haunted by remorseless furies ; and he had found healing in the calm nobility of Charlotte von Stein's presence, as Orestes in the presence of his sister. Here was the subjective motive from which the drama sprang. But we would do well not to overstrain what might be called the biographic interpretation of Goethe's work. Goethe's remark that all his works are but fragments of a great confession, has led to a tendency to fix the originals of the men and women of his books which can only be deprecated. There was some reason—although this too must be narrowly limited —for discovering portraits in the works of " Sturm und Drang," but after Goethe left the " Sturm und Drang " behind him, such identifications are often seriously misleading. To find the problem

of Orestes' life foreshadowed in the poet's own
experiences and trials, to say that traits in Iphigenia
herself were borrowed from the woman whose love
inspired Goethe's early Weimar years, is one thing :
it is another to say, as many of Goethe's critics
are inclined to do, that Orestes is Goethe, Iphigenia
Charlotte von Stein. Indeed, Iphigenia is most
emphatically not Charlotte ; there is more of the
classic tradition in her than of any flesh and blood
model. That very touch of superhuman priest-
hood with which Goethe has endowed her, that calm
that betrays no joy at seeing her lost brother, nor
sorrow at her mother's murder, is tradition, and
was not invented by Goethe.

Although we must be wary in explaining by
mere rule of thumb the infinite variety and subtlety
of a poet's relation to reality, we are at the same
time able to feel at once what in Goethe's poetry
is experienced and what is only invented. If this
feeling does not betray us in the present case, we
should say that Orestes alone is experienced ;
Iphigenie herself not at all, except perhaps in her
relation to Orestes' healing.

Or, to look at the problem of the drama in a wider,
more comparative spirit, what has Goethe attempted to do ? He has endeavoured to modern-
ise a Greek tragedy in the light of the philosophic
humanism, which suffused the whole century of

enlightenment. He has realised, as Schiller did later
in his classic tragedy *Die Braut von Messina*, the
incompatibility of Greek fatalism with the modern,
Christian conception of man's free will; and the
climax of his *Iphigenie* is brought about by an
act of free will on his heroine's part, which is
inconsistent with the fate-background. Had Goethe
still held to the uncompromising realism with which
he set out in life, *Iphigenie* might never have been
written. But Goethe here becomes an advocate of
the idea of moral regeneration so beloved of German
classical poetry. He will have us believe that the
innate nobility of his heroine's soul is alone sufficient
to disperse the Furies and heal Orestes, that—as he
summed the matter up in the motto of later years :
" pure humanity atones for every human frailty "
("jedes menschliche Gebrechen"). But does it,
or could it, unless in the eyes of an inveterate
optimist like Goethe ? To the modern mind the
story of Iphigenia is and only can be tragic : it is
true, Euripides avoids a tragic close : but it is
surely not too much to say that the instinct of the
Greek tragic poet would have preferred a tragic close
had tradition not decreed otherwise. As it is,
the Greek play ends ironically. But neither
Greek precedent nor common-sense realism could
have led a modern poet to choose deliberately
the improbable, artificial method Goethe has adopted

D

of bringing his drama to an end. Iphigenia here
asserts the power and majesty of the truth : she
cuts the tragic knot by being frank and straight-
forward : but in so doing she involves herself in a
risk, which in the whole history of tragedy has
never been known to avert the catastrophe; she
puts the gods to the test, and depends entirely
on their justifying her temerity. In other words
a mere chance, not the grim, eternal necessity
of Greek tragedy, brings Goethe's drama to a
conciliatory close.

This summary statement of modern critical
opinion on Goethe's *Iphigenie* points to the conclusion, that, however deeply we may fall under the
spell of this modern treatment of a Greek tragedy-
theme, we must seek in it no final solution
of the problem that will hold good for all time ;
but only an interpretation of it in the light of that
classic humanitarianism of which Goethe himself
is the greatest exponent. It is an eighteenth-century
interpretation of Greek tragedy, no more Greek
at bottom than the seventeenth-century interpre-
tations of the French stage, or, for that part, of
the realistic versions of the Greek drama in the
German theatre of to-day. Goethe's *Iphigenie*
remains an unmistakable product of an age of
humanitarian enlightenment.

After *Iphigenie* came *Tasso*, which belongs to a

distinctly later phase than its predecessor. Goethe, it might be said, did not go to Italy to finish *Iphigenie*, only to realise it : *Tasso*, on the other hand, was an actual product of Italy. What was written of it before Goethe saw Italy, was inconsiderable, at most the two first acts, and not all of them ; in its most essential elements it was conceived and planned in Rome, and it was not completed until after Goethe returned to Germany.

It would be idle to claim that *Tasso* is, in the judgment of modern Germany, a more vital play than *Iphigenie*. It is less frequently played upon the stage, and it is lacking in that perfection of form which we have described as the saving virtue of the earlier work. Superficially, and on a first reading, it would also seem to stand not much nearer to us to-day than *Iphigenie*. That drama had dealt with a well-worn theme and characters drawn from a remote antiquity, and presented them in the light of a social optimism, which was distinctly of the eighteenth century ; in *Tasso* Goethe gives us, against the background of the Italian Renaissance, a picture of the ripe culture and delicately harmonised etiquette of an eighteenth - century court—an etiquette which vanished from European society at the French Revolution, never to return again. This, it might seem, is hardly likely to make more appeal to us moderns than the conflict of

humane Greek and barbarian Scythian. But there
is a modern element in *Tasso* which especially
appeals to us now, and that is the extraordinarily
intimate subjectivity of its portraits. In this
courtly, old-world *milieu*, a very modern soul is
entrapped and imprisoned.

The story of Goethe's *Tasso* is almost as briefly
told as that of *Egmont*; indeed, it has no proper
dramatic action according to the traditional definition of what constitutes a plot. A supersensitive
poet is wounded in his *amour propre*, loses his
balance, and makes presumptuous love to a
princess, the sister of his patron ; he draws his
sword on an opponent, his patron's minister, ultimately to learn that the latter, the practical man of
the world, is his best friend. But just in respect
of this " actionless " plot, recent criticism seems
to have arrived at a fairer judgment than that of a
generation ago. It is becoming clear to us that
the whole development of the higher European
drama since Goethe has been in the direction foreshadowed by *Tasso* ; the theatre is learning to dis-
pense with visible happenings in favour of a
more subtle form of dramatic action, situation and
conflict, which takes place in the minds and souls
of the characters. A master-tragedy like Hebbel's
Gyges und sein Ring, or that most perfect, perhaps,
of all modern tragedies, Ibsen's *Rosmersholm*, has

little more action, in the accepted sense of the word, than *Torquato Tasso*. Indeed, viewed from this standpoint, Goethe's drama suffers, if anything from an excessive fullness of psychological movement.

But more serious reproaches have been brought against *Tasso* than its want of action. Almost every reader, who comes fresh to it, feels that it falls asunder into two halves which it is difficult to reconcile with each other ; in other words, that the drama which Goethe conceived in the pre-Italian days in Weimar, has not been successfully blended with the later development. The character of *Tasso's* opponent, Antonio Montecatino, seems lacking in consistency ; there are two Antonios who stand out quite distinctly from each other. But this confusion is probably due in great measure to the fact that the reader, mindful of the close where the poet resigns himself to the guidance and superior wisdom of the statesman, feels that Antonio ought throughout to enlist our full sympathy, which of course, he does not. Of all Goethe's contrast-figures, such as Carlos, Werner, Mephistopheles, none is more subtle and complicated than this ; but the subtlety is less due to the character itself than to the fact that it is varnished over with a polite court etiquette, which necessarily obscures the real man. The problem is, no doubt, simplified,

if, with some modern critics, we strip Antonio of
those idealising qualities which earlier opinion
attributed to him, and regard him as an unsympathetic and even cruel antagonist of Tasso ; let
us admit frankly that the last monologue in which
the poet clings like a ship-wrecked mariner to
Antonio, is only one more of the aberrations of
Tasso's life, that here too, disillusion will come
and come speedily. From such a point of view
—which, however, Goethe himself makes it very
difficult for us to adopt—the confusion in Antonio's
character and rôle no doubt disappears. The most
serious flaw of the drama, and the real difficulty, is
its close. It suffers under Goethe's imperturbable
optimism, suffers as *Faust, Egmont, Iphigenie* had
done. Strong and clear-headed as Goethe was,
he had not, as he himself confessed, the ruthlessness of the tragic poet, which lesser geniuses like
Schiller, Kleist, Grillparzer and Hebbel all possessed
in a higher degree. After *Werther* and *Clavigo*
Goethe never again braced himself to a real tragedy,
such as compels our fear and pity ; and none of
Goethe's greater works suffers more palpably from
this want of the tragic than *Tasso*. There was but
one ending to the embittered conflicts that are here
unrolled, conflicts unillumined by any spark of con-
solation, and that is the ending which history itself
offered ; had the doors of the madhouse closed on

Tasso instead of the poet leaving him clinging dis-
tractedly to a forlorn and elusive hope, Goethe's
drama would have gained infinitely in strength.
The healing of Tasso may have been the healing of
the poet Goethe in Italy, but we should have willingly
given this subjective touch in exchange for the
greater truth of *Werther*. The conflict is the same
here as in *Werther*, Goethe's one, real tragic conflict,
that of the sensitive, finely strung " superman," with
the unsympathetic world of reality. The unbalance
of the poet's soul is, as in *Werther*, the source of all
Tasso's suffering. Tasso is a calmer, maturer
Werther, for the poet himself had grown older and
wiser since those early days when a god had given
him so liberally " the power to say what he suffered."

In spite of Goethe's careful and often subtly
ingenious use of his Italian sources, there is little
that is historical about his *Tasso*. On the other
hand, there is more of Goethe's own self in Tasso
than in Orestes ; and there is at least a suggestion
of Karl August and the minister Fritsch in Alphons
and Antonio. But here again we must be careful
not to carry such analogies too far. What Goethe
has given us is no mere copy of reality ; and it is
impossible to take stock of the thousand and one
factors that blend and group themselves in a poet's
mind before they emerge in the form of creative
work. It is enough to say that in this poem Goethe

has produced the most wonderful drama of a sensitive poet's conflicts that the literature of the world has to show ; he has sounded depths which poetry had not before attempted to sound.

While in *Iphigenie* and *Tasso*, we see the ripe product of what Italy meant for Goethe's art as a poet, we have to turn to another work to see what might be called the ethic results of the Italian journey, namely, to *Wilhelm Meister*. It has been claimed for this novel that it contains the quintessence of Goethe's wisdom acquired in Italy. This is true, but by wisdom we must understand the practical wisdom of life, not the peculiar wisdom that makes the artist great. *Wilhelm Meister*, however, shares with *Egmont* the characteristic of having been very fully written at a much earlier period ; and it was not taken in hand again until some years after Goethe had returned from Italy. Its publication was contemporary with the beginning of Goethe's friendship with Schiller.

There is no work of Goethe's in the case of which it is so difficult to arrive at a final judgment as *Wilhelm Meister*. One has only to recall the extraordinarily varied and contradictory judgments of the last century, the passionate appreciation of the early romanticists and the cynical indifference of " Young Germany " ; or amongst ourselves, the valiant defence of Carlyle and the disparaging sneers of De Quincey. That a work should awaken such warm partisanship for and against, such enthusiastic admiration and such antagonism, is in itself a testimony that it possesses the germinative qualities of great literature ; it is all the more reason that we should face the problem of its place in literature once more.

From the point of view of literary art *Meister* has many and grave shortcomings. Goethe himself did not by any means regard it as perfect ; he complained, in the days when Scott was attracting the eyes of all Europe, that he had had no romantic Scotland to draw upon when he wrote his novel ; not realising that it was he himself in his own romantic days who had pointed out the way which Scott followed. But modern criticism is hardly likely to regard it as a shortcoming of *Wilhelm Meister* that it has nothing of the romantic halo of the *Waverley Novels*. Like so many of the poet's greater works, it suffered under the length of time it was in the making, and under the consequent change of plan. This is the real source of its weakness. Not only was the time-gap between the plan and the final completion a wide one ; but a novel, unlike a drama, does not admit of the same complete revisal ; it is impossible to bring all its complicated ramifications, its incidents, its style, into line. Consequently the want of unity is more apparent and disturbing. There is reason for believing that the inception of the romance dates back to that intensely productive period of Goethe's life, his Frankfort years ; that *Wilhelm Meister* was conceived immediately after *Werther*. However that may be, it was, at least in its first form, to be a novel about the theatre, and the " Sturm und Drang " had forced this institution into the forefront of contemporary interest as never before. A lucky accident has preserved for us Goethe's novel, if not perhaps in its very first plan, at least in the form in which Goethe brought it to a conclusion a year or two after he settled in Weimar ; and this early version makes clear that *Wilhelm Meister* was begun quite frankly as a novel of the theatre. This fact exonerates the excessive technical detail with which the theatre is discussed, a detail including, however, as we must gratefully acknowledge, the masterly criticism of *Hamlet*, which has formed one of the starting-points for modern Shakespeare exegesis.

When Goethe resumed work on his novel after a pause of some seventeen or eighteen years, the theatre had no longer the first place in his interests, while his thoughts on the serious problems of life had gained in depth. *Wilhelm Meisters Lehrjahre* ceased to be, in the first instance, the story of an amateur's apprenticeship to the art of the theatre,

and become the apprenticeship of a young man to
the most difficult of all arts, the art of living. The
centre of gravity passed from the æsthetic to the
moral. Moreover, the general venue of the work
had widened ; it was no longer limited to the free
and easy life of wandering actors in contrast with
the staid respectability of the man of business.
Goethe attempted a completer picture of eighteenth-
century society with its sharply drawn dividing
lines ; he introduced a contrast—and Goethe is
always admirable in drawing contrasting *milieus*—
more vital to the century than that of artist and
burgher, by bringing together burgher and aristo-
crat ; and between these two *milieus* Wilhelm
moves to and fro. His education is completed
by contact with them. Like Saul, the son of Kish,
he had gone out to find his father's asses, namely,
the art of the theatre ; what he did find was the
kingdom of life.

But however we may appreciate the ethical
deepening of the work, we are justified in the criticism that the book has suffered artistically by the
superposition of ideas originally foreign to it. The
best parts are undoubtedly those delightfully fresh
descriptions of Wilhelm's doings among his actor
friends. The new element, which bulks most
largely in the revised novel of 1796, the aristocratic
element, is disappointing. Here all is shadowy ;

the Lotharios and Aurelies and Nathalies are the merest paper creations, shadows like the anæmic personages of quite subordinate works of the poet, such as the *Unterhaltungen deutscher Ausgewanderten*. Their introduction may have brought variety into the picture, and meant a widening of the ethic problem and scope; but they are no artistic gain. Whatever Italy did for Goethe, whatever ripeness it brought, it seems to have effectually destroyed this peculiar creative faculty. Moreover, the closing books are supplemented unnecessarily by the *Bekenntnisse einer schönen Seele*, a kind of padding to which Goethe, as the years crept on him, became increasingly addicted; and the freemasonry with which the book closes appears to us now only unreal and tedious.

But there is something enigmatic about this vari-coloured work, something that always evades our grasp. We have no sooner satisfied ourselves by condemning its artistic formlessness and want of plan, than other aspects force themselves on our notice and compel us to return to the novel once more. It may be made up of the most ill-assorted shreds and patches; but we have to confess that some of these shreds and patches, judged by themselves, are extraordinarily beautiful; it may be full of contradictory, or seemingly contradictory ideas on human morals—taking seriously what we consider should not be taken seriously, and the reverse—but it gradually begins to dawn on us that, in spite of its preoccupation with actors and idlers, it contains more vital ideas about the conduct of life in its widest and most serious aspects than any other work of fiction. *Wilhelm Meister* is, once more, an illustration of that persistent interest which clings to works of genius with all manner of loose ends and unsatisfied issues. It would be difficult to point to another novel of the eighteenth century, or, indeed, of the earlier nine-teenth century, which has still such a well-justified claim on the attention of the modern world as this.

That *Wilhelm Meister* is Germany's representative novel there can be no manner of doubt. It seems to us now a kind of goal towards which the German fiction of the eighteenth century was unconsciously working ; and the whole subsequent development of German fiction, through the dream-like fancies of the Romantic School to the modern social novel of Freytag, Spielhagen, and Heyse, after the middle of the nineteenth century, stands under the ban of Goethe's novel. The fact that, in spite of the powerful influences of French and English fiction, and, at a later date, of Russian, the German novel has been able to maintain a distinct national stamp, to retain its subjectivity and disregard for " well-constructed " plots—qualities which we so often unthinkingly condemn, because they do not happen to be French, bears testimony to the dominant power of Goethe's example.

CHAPTER V

THE FRIENDSHIP OF GOETHE AND SCHILLER;
GOETHE'S CLASSICISM

THE friendship of Goethe and Schiller, which continued unbroken and in a steady crescendo from the year 1794 to Schiller's death in 1805, is one of the most attractive episodes in modern literary history. At the first glance it would seem to belong rather to the might-have-beens of literature than to its realities that the two greatest poets of a nation should be thus bound together in the best years of their lives by a sincere and generous intimacy. One thinks of Goethe and Schiller as in the statue before the Court Theatre in Weimar standing hand in hand, the two leading poets of their generation, separated by a wide gulf from their contemporaries, united in alliance against the petty philistines, their common foe, and the sworn enemies of

Was uns alle bändigt, das Gemeine.

This period in the lives of Goethe and Schiller is enshrined in one of the most precious books of the German classic age, the *Correspondence between Schiller and Goethe*, which Goethe published in 1827.

The peculiar value of these letters is the fact that
they afford us glimpses into the workshops of the
two men, into their mind and art as poets, and
supplement those admirable treatises of Schiller's in
which the literary and æsthetic ideals of the age were
formulated. Both poets had arrived at that level
plateau of middle life when the unrest of youth
is over, when plans are clearly defined and the
unexpected no longer awakens disconcerting surprise. Theirs was essentially a sober friendship,
an intellectual companionship ; the passionate con-
fidences of youth were no longer possible ; and an
inner sanctuary in each poet's life was always kept
sacredly veiled from the other. The intimate personal tone which Schiller adopted towards Körner,
and Goethe even towards so late a friend as Zelter,
is absent. This aloofness in matters of personal
intimacy is more noticeable in Goethe ; even when
he writes of literary matters, he is rarely discursive
on his own work and plans. Schiller is disposed
to be more communicative, but—in the earlier
stages at least—he is a little overawed by his
friend's greatness ; and Goethe does little towards
putting him at his ease. One may even detect
a tendency on the younger poet's part to hero-
worship and incense-burning, as in the devotion
with which he reads and eulogises *Wilhelm Meister*,
a work which we can hardly imagine would appeal

so warmly to him as his letters imply. And Goethe
accepts everything as his right, and in a tone often
bordering on patronage. As the years moved on
the intimacy increased ; but of the most intimate
period, when both poets lived in Weimar, the correspondence has virtually nothing to tell us, for the
need of writing letters had ceased.

At the outset of their friendship Goethe and
Schiller made the discovery that, in spite of their
very different temperaments, they did not stand at
such irreconcilable extremes as they had believed ;
and the repeated attacks of a petty, materialistic
criticism, to which both alike were exposed, brought
them closer. They routed their enemies in their
Xenien, and then, in friendly rivalry, enriched German
classical poetry with a series of ballads of rare
beauty and classic form. Having thus found
their way back to the poetic fold, the desire came
to both to try their strength in greater works of
literary art. Schiller set to work on *Wallenstein* ;
Goethe wrote *Hermann und Dorothea*. The incal-
culable value of the mutual friendship was that it
brought both men away from more or less alien
fields, from philosophy, history, science, to the one
art in which they stood on common ground, the
art of poetry. Since his return from Italy Goethe
had stood aloof from literature, like a sullen Achilles ;
while Schiller was lost in the mazes of the Kantian

E

philosophy. To Goethe we owe the stimulus that has given us the varicoloured series of Schiller's dramas from *Wallenstein* to *Wilhelm Tell*; to Schiller, not merely Goethe's *Hermann und Dorothea* and *Die natürliche Tochter*, but, most precious of all, the completion of the First Part of *Faust*.

Before turning to these poems, we must look for a moment at Goethe's life between his return from Italy and the composition of these works. Besides *Tasso* and *Wilhelm Meister*, works which in the previous chapter have been brought into connection with the Italian journey, Goethe made an admirable version in hexameters of the masterpiece of Low German literature, *Reineke Fuchs*; he polished and perfected the wonderful *Römische Elegien*, blending their note of Southern passion with his love for his new friend in Weimar, Christiane Vulpius. These little poems, perhaps the most unGerman of the whole classic age, form an even more personal confession of the Italianate Goethe than the larger works that have already been considered. And in 1790 he endeavoured, with, however, less success, to give these *Elegies* a successor in the *Venezianische Epigramme*. In the main, Goethe was immersed from the early nineties onwards, in scientific pursuits, and he attached more importance to his quest of a formula that should refute the Newtonian theory of light, establish the aqueous origin of the earth's crust, or demonstrate morphological unity in plants and anatomical continuity in the higher mammals, than to literary work. Poetry was but the occupation of his leisure moments, and, for the most part, not even that. When we follow in detail the records of the poet's diaries and correspondence in these years, we realise how much the modern reader, who prizes the poet Goethe above all else, owes to Schiller.

Hermann und Dorothea has been frequently described as Goethe's most perfect poem; it is at least his most perfect classic one. It is the direct outcome of those discussions of classic art which take up so large a part of the correspondence in 1797 and 1798; it is a carefully planned adaptation to German conditions of the style and art of the *Iliad* and the *Odyssey*. Goethe's hexameters are not, of course, Greek hexameters, still less Klopstock's; they are an adaptation of the Greek hexameter to modern German needs and German rhythmic feeling. There is nothing Greek about the theme; it is nationally German, and brought skilfully into touch with the great event that filled men's minds in these years, the French Revolution. The story itself was originally about Salzburg emigrants; Goethe transfers the scene to the Rhine. Hermann, the son of the Landlord of the " Golden Lion " in a German village, finds his

bride among a party of fugitives from the other side
of the Rhine, fugitives from the anarchy and horrors
of France. This slight story is symmetrically
shaped and modelled, and apportioned into nine
cantos, each of which bears the name of a Greek
muse. Over the whole lies a fine veil of harmonious style, which eliminates from the story the
crude reality of actual happenings ; the idealisation
of a placid, optimistic art invades every corner
and cranny of the picture. The repugnance to
reality, which had now become the corner-stone of
Goethe's and Schiller's creed, is most noticeable in
the characters of *Hermann und Dorothea*. They
are all generalised according to principles and
by methods similar to those which the Cartesian
philosophy had imposed upon the literature of the
French *grand siècle*. Hermann is no clearly drawn,
unique individual, as Egmont had been, or Clavigo,
—no subjective portrait of Goethe's own self,
like Werther ; he is, so to speak, not *a* German
youth, but *the* German youth, a composite portrait
formed from an infinite number of more or less representative individuals. In the same way Dorothea,
whom it is unwise to associate too closely, as some
critics have done, with Lili, is carefully freed from
all individualising features. Even had Lili stood
in the background of Goethe's mind, when he drew
Dorothea, there is much less of her here than there

is of Frau von Stein in his *Iphigenie*. The Landlord of the Golden Lion and his spouse are types; even the Apothecary, the most striking figure of all, is typically conceived. The scene is an idealised German village; and the poet himself would no doubt have repudiated any attempt, such as that recently made by an American scholar, to identify his locality.

Thus in all that concerns form, technique, and aim, *Hermann und Dorothea* is a wholly classical poem. In his lifetime Goethe went through three clearly marked phases of classicism, which correspond roughly with the general development of European classicism in the eighteenth century. In Leipzig he began as an adept in a purely French classicism or pseudo-classicism; his second phase is the classicism of *Iphigenie* and *Tasso*, which, in spite of somewhat questionable pseudo-classic origins, was chastened and purified by the teaching of Winkelmann, and, above all, by Italy; but this phase was still compatible with a very considerable infusion of subjectivity, and aimed rather at classic restfulness than at symmetry of classic form and classic generalisation. The third phase, that of *Hermann und Dorothea*, was born in great measure of theory; it is the culmination of a carefully built-up classic art, from which the intractable element of the naïve has been completely eliminated.

But just in this lack of *naïveté* lies a source of weakness for a poet like Goethe, whose supremely great work is naïve. It was not Goethe's *métier* to work according to theories ; and his work under such conditions lapsed—as, for instance, Schiller's never did—into artificiality. With all its perfection there is a certain coldness about *Hermann und Dorothea*, which makes it less precious to us to-day than the more living creations of Goethe's " Sturm und Drang." If the world has to choose between work that is formless and extravagant, but true, and work in which the perfection of form is due to an artificial construction that smacks of theory, it will usually decide in favour of the former.

Moreover, by one of those strokes of irony which lend dramatic interest to literary history, there arose in Berlin and Jena a new literary school, the Romantic School, in the very year in which this masterpiece of German classic art appeared. The young Romantic movement was a protest against the classic idealism of Goethe and Schiller, and, as time went on, it suffused with an anti-classic individualism the whole poetic life of the new century.   The two friends, however, were not so easily turned from their path ; they persisted for a few years longer in their endeavours to establish a Græco-German art, carrying their theories to still more uncompromising extremes.   In *Die Braut von Messina* Schiller measured himself with the Greek poets in their own domain, and in *Die natürliche Tochter* Goethe produced a play of the French Revolution on the severest classical and impersonal lines. He even avoided giving his characters names, lest the sanctity of type should be disturbed by the intrusion of individualising traits ; the last drop of that subjectivity which was the life-blood of *Götz* and *Werther* has been squeezed out. The drama of *Pandora*, which did not, however, appear till 1810, is even a step further on this same path, but then *Pandora* is frankly an allegory ; the subtleties of its poetic symbolism place it outside such criticism as we are justified in using of *Die natürliche Tochter*. The time, however, soon came when both Goethe and Schiller realised that the path they had chosen would ultimately divorce them wholly from the literature of their people. They gave up the quest of the Greek ideal ; *Die Braut von Messina* was followed by *Wilhelm Tell*, *Die natürliche Tochter* by *Faust*. With the appearance of the First Part of *Faust* all Goethe's classical aberrations were forgiven him : *Faust* was hailed as the crowning work of the national literature.

The death of Schiller, in 1805, made a break in the even tenor of Goethe's life. In losing Schiller Goethe felt that he had been deprived of one of his main supports ; even if Schiller's lofty, unworldly

idealism, that " lost itself in the sky," was far removed
from that realistic attitude which the older poet,
in spite of his Greek theories, could not disavow,
there was something inspiring and stimulating in
living in intimate proximity to such an idealism.
This, at least, is what we read out of that magnificent poetic tribute which Goethe paid his friend in
his *Epilog zu Schillers Glocke*.

Tasso has been described above as Goethe's
most modern drama ; one might in the same way
single out *Die Wahlverwandtschaften* (" The Elective
Affinities "), which appeared in 1809, as his most
modern novel, the novel which is most in sympathy
with recent developments of literature. *Die Wahlverwandtschaften* is a purely psychological study, a
forerunner of those probings into the emotional
workings of the soul which have distinguished
the masterpieces of Russian and French fiction
in the past hundred years. But it is modern, too,
even in the superficialities of theme and treatment ;
it discusses with a seriousness unknown to the
eighteenth century, problems of marriage and sex,
and makes an effort to explain on psychological, not
sentimental, grounds the problems it raises. Goethe
approaches his theme as a scientific observer ; he
arranges an experiment in sex-attraction, as a
pathologist intent on establishing new laws, and,
note-book in hand, he registers each phase in the

experiment. As a chemist might place four elements
together and observe them follow out their natural
affinities, so Goethe here brings together, two men
and two women. The love which had in earlier
years drawn Eduard and Charlotte together, has
gradually died out; the circumstances of their lives
had forced them to form other ties ; and now,
in later life when they find themselves free to marry,
they are brought together by old associations rather
than love. The bond that unites them is, as it
were, sufficiently loose to leave them open to find
other affinities. And these appear in a military
captain who joins their circle, and Ottilie, Charlotte's
young foster-daughter. These four human beings
are Goethe's materials, and now he stands aside
and watches what happens. It is unfortunate that
so well-planned and interesting an experiment in
life and manners should suffer from what we have
called the anæmic qualities common to all Goethe's
post-Italian creations. The figures of the novel
resemble, in their shadowy unreality, those of the
later books of *Wilhelm Meisters Lehrjahre*. The theme
and problems were worthy of a better framework
than that which Goethe has given them ; there is
something repellently artificial about the development of the story ; it is constructed like the estate
on which Eduard and the Captain lavish so much
thought, that is to say, it is a conscious imitation of

nature, which only conveys the impression that it is *not* nature. It must be admitted, too, that, as the book progressed, Goethe shirked its difficulties ; instead of weaving character and ideas into one whole, he has recourse to wearisome expedients, such as a diary. His wisdom had deepened and his intellectual horizon had widened, but the artist in Goethe had to pay for the gain. We read *Die Wahlverwandtschaften* now, as we read *Wilhelm Meisters Wanderjahre*, less for the pleasure to be derived from it as a work of art than for its ideas. In the same way, all the ripe wisdom in the additions to the First Part of *Faust* cannot hold the balance with the naïve realism which makes the *Urfaust* one of the most wonderful examples of spontaneous creation in the literature of the world.

In after years Goethe laid great store by the subjective element in his novel. " There is not a stroke in the *Wahlverwandtschaften*," he said to Eckermann, " that I have not myself experienced, but none exactly as it has been experienced." And although the post-Italian Goethe was but little disposed, or able, to make direct confessions in his books, there is truth in this statement ; rightly read, the novel is an intimate confession of Goethe's own psychological experiences as a lover and a husband. Even its conclusions are flesh and blood of Goethe himself ; for although *Die Wahlverwandtschaften* is a scientific experiment, it is, like all experimentation in the infancy of modern science, an experiment with the very definite purpose of proving an hypothesis. In other words, the novel has its " lesson." It is a demonstration of the majesty of nature's laws, a vindication of morality exemplified by a tragedy of uncontrolled passion, a " Tendenzschrift " against the laxity of the Romantic School and a protest against moral anarchy. Once more Goethe states, from still another point of view, the basic principle of his own rule of conduct : the salvation of erring man can only be attained through steadfast strength of will and purpose, through the power to " renounce." It is in this idea that the ethic strength of the book has to be sought, just as its value as a work of art lies in its emphasis of the psychological. And in both aspects it was a book of the future, rather than of its own time.

CHAPTER VI

THE LAST TWENTY YEARS

GOETHE's old age was, as old age usually is, un-eventful. Apart from the publication of occasional new books and new editions of early ones, its main events were the severing by death of old ties, ties that could not be replaced by new ones. In this period we are supplied with a fullness of information about the poet's life, as never before ; his correspondence was more voluminous than ever, and every fragment of writing coming from so famous a man was carefully garnered and preserved; he was sur-rounded by friends who worshipped him and reverently recorded every word that fell from his lips ; and, as if this were not enough, he himself kept his diary with a fullness and detail for which there had been no time in earlier years. The fierce light that beats on intellectual thrones was never fiercer than in Weimar during the first thirty years of the nineteenth century. A lesser man might have come badly out of such an ordeal of publicity ; but no one can say that Goethe did not grow old with dignity. Perhaps, indeed, there was just a little too much dignity—a dignity that occasionally conveyed a false impression of Goethe's real self. With each year the circle of Goethe's friends and correspondents widened : travellers from every land of Europe visited the great man and put on record how he received them. He had left much of his pre-Revolutionary thought and feeling behind, but to one eighteenth-century dream he remained faithful to the last—cosmopolitanism ; as a champion of a " world literature," that was hemmed in by no narrowing political frontiers, Goethe entered readily into correspondence with the poets and men of letters of other lands. Indeed, so warmly did he welcome the genius of foreigners like Byron, Scott, and Manzoni, that critics at home were not unjustified in feeling a certain jealousy.

Goethe grew old unwillingly, one might even say with difficulty. His heart, his emotional sensitiveness, kept him strangely young, even after his hair was white, and his outward dealing with men had taken on a formality that seemed inconsistent with lyric effusiveness. But in 1811 he himself took a step, which showed that he realised that the years were accumulating on his shoulders ; he made a beginning to that summation of his life and activity which he felt was demanded of him by mankind, by collecting materials for his autobiography. It is trite to speak nowadays in superlatives of Goethe's *Dichtung und Wahrheit* ; it is no doubt still Goethe's most popular and generally read prose work ; the greatest confession of one whose whole literary work was one long confession. What Goethe meant by his title is still not altogether clear. Do the words " Dichtung " and " Wahrheit " mean that he intentionally set out to romance about himself, as for instance Bettina von Arnim romanced about him in her delightful book *Goethe's Correspondence with a Child* ? Are we to take Goethe's account of himself as in parts an intentional perversion of facts ? Whatever Goethe meant by " Dichtung," it has now been abundantly proved that it was not this. Goethe gave himself infinite pains to present as true and faithful a picture of himself as he could ; he had no intention to conceal the truth or to beautify it. But looking back through thirty and forty years, events, tinged with the light of retrospect, assumed no doubt in his mind an aspect which was not in exact accordance with the truth. The picture we obtain from contemporary letters and doctrines does not always correspond to the softened contours of the autobiography ; the young Goethe's joys were more tumultuous, his enthusiasms more heaven-scaling, his griefs more poignant than he would have us believe. There were harshnesses and crudities in reality which are here unintentionally toned down ; but the actual facts were not essentially different from what Goethe believed them to be.

It is doubtful, however, if this introduction of the factor of retrospect was what the poet had in view when he used the expression " Dichtung." What he meant was rather that he subjected the story of his life to a process not unsimilar to that which, in a higher degree, he had submitted the material with which he had dealt as a poet. He applied to his life the teleological methods of the historians of the eighteenth century : he interpreted events, that is to say, in the light of the one far-off event towards which all things seemed to move. " Dichtung " meant that, instead of putting down the facts in the empiric, unreasoning way in which all facts occur, he grouped them, ordered them, interpreted them, as so many stages in the evolution of a man of genius. He wrote of his youth as one who knew the ripe achievement of the life that followed. It was this subjection of reality to the harmonising interpretation of the poet, this subordination of the parts to the whole, that constituted Goethe's "-fiction." And it is just in this ingredient, added by the artist in Goethe, that the perpetual charm of his work lies. Rousseau's *Confessions*, with its harsh record of facts, may be a more faithful record of the eighteenth-century mind and the eighteenth-century outlook on life ; but the *Confessions* is no longer a living book in the twentieth century as Goethe's autobiography is.

We cannot but regret that Goethe did not carry
his work beyond his early Frankfort years. It
has been suggested that he felt reluctant to write
of times and people so much nearer to him ; more
probably he felt a difficulty in discovering the
precise form of " Dichtung " which would throw the
facts of his Weimar life into the light he required.
We have, it is true, a kind of surrogate for the continuation in other documents, such as the *Italienische
Reise* and the many volumes of Diaries and Correspondence ; but in spite of this, as all readers of
Goethe's biography feel, that secret of higher inter-
pretative truth has not yet been found that will
bring Goethe's Weimar life into harmony with the
period that preceded it.

From the closely woven background of Goethe's
old age stand out three works of supreme interest,
in which Goethe once more showed his skill in the
three chief forms of modern literary art, the lyric,
the novel, and the drama. These works are *Der
Westöstliche Divan* (1819), *Wilhelm Meisters Wanderjahre* (1821-29), and the Second Part of *Faust* (1832).
But these books by no means exhaust Goethe's
activity in these later years. To his manifold
scientific interests and his penetrating criticism
we shall return in a subsequent chapter ; and even
his minor literary work in this epoch is significant.
Many modern readers will, indeed, turn rather to

byways of Goethe's activity than to the larger works ;
repelled by the socialistic philosophy of the *Wanderjahre*, or the allegory of the Second *Faust*, they
may still find an inexhaustible source of interest
and inspiration in the concentrated wisdom of the
Zahme Xenien and the *Sprüche in Prosa*.

Der Westöstliche Divan represents the Indian
summer of Goethe's lyric and emotional nature.
It is a defiant protest against the encroachment of
the years. Once more, at the age of sixty-five,
the lyric chord in Goethe was touched by a new
love, that for Marianne von Willemer, and his
feelings found vent in a new lyric vehicle, the oriental
poetic form of the Persian poet, Hafiz. The
spontaneity of Goethe's first period cannot be
claimed for the lyrics of the *Westöstliche Divan* ; it
was not given to Goethe after his journey to Italy,
to pour out his feelings as in earlier days. Perhaps,
too, it is unfair to him to emphasise the amatory
side of this interest which Marianne von Willemer
inspired in him ; what has already been said of the
peculiar, half-fictitious character of Goethe's various
love-affairs is particularly applicable to the present
case. The " Dichtung " predominates over the
" Wahrheit " ; the fiction of the oriental singer is a
real fiction, and not merely a veil behind which stands
Goethe himself. Hatem, the lover, is not Goethe ;
he is a creation apart from Goethe, as Faust is, or

F

Wilhelm Meister, or Tasso ; Goethe observes the
working of passion in him, as he had observed it
in the characters of his *Wahlverwandtschaften*, and
puts the results of his observations on record ;
of the *Divan*, too, he might say there is " not a
stroke in it which has not been experienced," but
" not a stroke that has been experienced just as
here described." Another interesting feature about
this book is the concession it makes to the new
Romantic movement. Goethe, as we have seen, had
stood nominally apart from the young individualists
who made so brave a stand against the stiffening
classicism of Weimar ; but his was a Protean nature
and extremely sensitive to the charm of novelty. He
could not follow the advancing Romantic movement into occultism, and into excesses that recalled
the " Sturm und Drang " of his own youth, nor
had he much sympathy for the enthusiasm for
oppressed nationalities like the Poles and the Greeks ;
but the Romantic orientalism of Hafiz he could
appreciate, and his *Divan* is in this respect a very
genuine enrichment of Romantic literature.

In 1821 appeared the first volume of the long-
expected continuation of *Wilhelm Meister, Wilhelm
Meisters Wanderjahre, oder die Entsagenden*. But
not for the first time in Goethe's life, not even for
the first time in the history of this particular novel,
Goethe had dallied too long. The real continuation

of the *Lehrjahre* could only have been written
immediately after the completion of that work ;
it is essentially a novel of the pre-Revolutionary
régime, a novel which reproduces the social conditions and ideas of the eighteenth century. A
continuation written in the nineteenth century
had, of necessity, to be a new work. The Wilhelm
who in the first part completes his apprenticeship
to life, was obviously totally unfitted to continue
his " Wanderjahre " in the new century ; for that
an entirely different kind of apprenticeship was
demanded. The dilettantism of the theatre, the
trite contrast of the idealising artist and the hidebound man of business, the polite insincerities
of a pre-Revolutionary aristocratic culture, were no
preparation at all for the hero who had now to face
nineteenth-century problems of human life and
destiny. *Wilhelm Meisters Wanderjahre*, as originally planned in Goethe's mind, could not be written
in 1821 ; and Goethe soon realised this. He made
a beginning, but the old world was not to be brought
to life again ; the figures receded into schematic
vagueness and unreality ; their human relations interested Goethe himself little, and they hardly interest
us at all. By their very ineffectualness they made
the necessary break with the first part; and that break
being made, Goethe probably felt freer to make the
book a mere vehicle for ideas and abstractions. The

Wanderjahre contains his most advanced political
thought and the most succinct statement of his
views on religion ; but that these ideas are expressed
in connection with the Wilhelm Meister of the early
nineties of the previous century, that the " pedagogic province " is created to educate that Wilhelm's
son, means as little to us as that the Faust of the
Second Part of that poem once loved Gretchen.
It is difficult nowadays to discover what Goethe
originally intended to do with his hero on his
" Wanderjahre " ; possibly he himself no longer
knew, when he took up the thread again.   In any
case, the continuation of Goethe's novel remains
the most fragmentary and unsatisfactory of all his
continuations.   The material was not even adequate
for his purpose, and he supplemented it by the
introduction of much irrelevant matter, short stories
of small literary quality, which had been written
in no connection with *Wilhelm Meister* and are
merely introduced to fill out the volumes.

But Goethe's career was not destined to taper
thus ineffectually to an end.   In all the years since
Schiller had first given him the stimulus, *Faust*
had not been forgotten ; it moved steadily forward,
accompanying Goethe like that mirror borne along
the highway of life, to which Stendhal likened the
modern novel.   The poetic transmutation of his
spiritual life in this last period found its way into

the Second Part ; and it is to us now only one more
proof of the providential fate that favoured Goethe
all his life long, that he should have been spared
to put the finishing touches to this, the crowning
work of his life.

When Goethe died, on March 22, 1832, it seemed
to contemporaries as if an era in the world's history
had closed, as if a new era in European thought and
poetry had begun. The magnitude of Goethe's
life-work it is perhaps even still difficult to gauge.
He has left behind him a library of books bearing
his name, greater than that even of Voltaire, and of
greater variety ; more than this, he has called into
being a vast literature about himself and his work
of which the end is not yet. His long life goes
back to the pseudo-classic era of Gottsched, ranges
through Lessing's classicism, the new-birth of
individualism with Rousseau and Herder, to the
German " Sturm und Drang " whose leader and
idol he became. And from " Sturm und Drang "
Goethe led his literature back into calmer waters,
back to a serene classicism, and a wide-hearted
humanitarianism, in which the movement of the
eighteenth century found its goal. Judged thus,
Goethe is the continuer and perfecter of that great
movement of humanism which, inaugurated by the
Italian Renaissance, brought to each nation in
Europe in turn, to Italy, to France, to Germany,

its flourishing period ; to Goethe it was reserved to
give the movement of the Renaissance its last and
highest form. But this does not by any means
exhaust Goethe's significance for the literature of
Germany and of Europe. Had his life been cut
short, as Schiller's was, in the zenith of classicism,
it would be easier for us to-day to close the records
over him, to round off and sum up his life. But
Goethe belonged to two centuries, and came to an
understanding with the nineteenth century as no other
thinker or poet whose most impressionable years
had been lived in the pre-Revolutionary era.
More than a third of his long life was passed in
the midst of the individualistic revival we know
to-day as German Romanticism, the movement
which succeeded and to some extent superseded
Weimar classicism. And towards this movement
Goethe's attitude was one of understanding and en-
couragement. He greeted and admired Byron, Scott
and Carlyle ; his sympathies went out to the young
Romantic dreamers who were preparing a great era
for the literature of France, and to the Romanticists
of Italy. Goethe, the poet of eighteenth-century
Classicism, was also a poet of nineteenth-century
Romanticism. He who had begun in the school
of Leibniz and Wolff, who had grown up with
Rousseau, lived through the period of Kant to
that of Hegel, even of Schopenhauer. The poet

whose ripest years were reached when the great Revolution broke over France lived long enough to see that other, less sanguinary, but spiritually hardly less significant, Revolution of July 1830, which broke the domination of Romanticism in European letters, and led poetry back into channels other than Romantic.

CHAPTER VII

" FAUST "

FOR those who will see Goethe's vast activity as a whole, the course here adopted of reserving his *Faust* for discussion in a chapter by itself may seem difficult to justify ; such readers might prefer to have the chief work of the poet's life woven into the texture of his biography, and instead of one *Faust*, have presented to them the three *Fausts*, that of Goethe's youth, of his middle-age and his old-age, each differentiated and set by itself. And, remembering what has been said of Goethe's life as the supremely interesting thing about him, their demand has a certain justification. On the other hand, something may be urged in favour of looking at the poem as the poet himself intended it to be looked at, as one indivisible whole, not as a record of personal phases, and we are especially justified in doing so by the fact that to the modern English reader *Faust* is Goethe. To know *Faust* is one of the most elementary and obvious duties of modern culture, even if our knowledge of Goethe begins and ends with that work.

Faust, like every great poetic creation, may be

regarded from two points of view, the subjective
or personal one, that is to say, in its relations to the
poet himself, and the objective one, in its relations
to the literary movement of its time. Both these
aspects of Goethe's drama are alike interesting.
Faust is the work of Goethe's whole lifetime ; its
beginnings date back to his earliest literary ambi-
tions, and the finishing touches were put to the
Second Part only a few months before he died.
It is thus in quite a unique sense the poetic
record of Goethe's emotional and intellectual life.
At what date he first resolved to make the old story
the subject of a tragedy it is difficult to say, but we
shall doubtless not be far wrong if we accept the
statement of *Dichtung und Wahrheit* that Götz
von Berlichingen and Faust were the two figures
which had the first place in the poet's heart in
those eventful months he passed as a student in
Strassburg in 1770 and 1771. " The significant
puppet-play of *Faust* hummed and echoed in me
in many tones. I, too, had wandered in all fields
of knowledge, and had early come to see the vanity
of them all. I had tried all kinds of ways in life,
and had always returned more dissatisfied and
troubled." Older memories from Frankfort and
Leipzig were embodied in the poem, but its real
birthplace was Strassburg, even if, as seems likely
to have been the case, Goethe's preoccupation with

Götz von Berlichingen left him but little time to give
his ideas shape, until he returned to Frankfort.
Here, between 1773 and 1775, he worked at the
drama in earnest.

The most striking features of this *Urfaust*, as
the early Frankfort version has been called, are its
imaginative strength and the unity of its style.
Fragmentary it may be, but it comes all from one
mould.   Goethe poured all his own personal " Storm
and Stress " into his hero.   He fixed in this *Faust* a
definite phase in his development, and that with such
abundance of subjective detail that any remoulding
or continuation in later years had of necessity to
appear as supererogatory patchwork. ·A simple
human tragedy of overpowering pathos, this early
Faust is the greatest achievement of Goethe's
youth.   There is nothing philosophical in it, no
self-conscious wrestling with the enigmas of existence ; even the problems which the old " Volksbuch "
suggested are evaded.   Mephistopheles, so far from
being the philosophical devil with a mission, which
he subsequently became, is merely the incarnation of a popular idea, an emissary of evil, who,
by means Goethe did not take time to tell us about,
has got Faust into his meshes and succeeds in
wrecking his life and Gretchen's.   Obviously the
young poet was more interested in his lovers than
in his devil, and he unfolds their fate with a tragic

power which no other European poet of his time
possessed ; the scene entitled later " Trüber Tag,
Feld " is one of the most concentrated pieces of
dramatic writing in the literature of the world.

It seems necessary, in view of the many volumes
that have been written on the philosophic bearings
of Goethe's *Faust*, to emphasise the absolutely
unmetaphysical nature of its beginnings. There is
an undoubted danger among *Faust* commentators
to refine and philosophise overmuch. Goethe in
his own day had to protest ; and it seems still more
necessary to protest now. What makes *Faust* the
greatest work in the German tongue is, after all,
not its philosophy, but its art, its imagination, its
poetry ; and these qualities more immediately
appeal to us in this early form, because the later
philosophic ideas have not yet been superimposed
on them. The strength of Goethe's Mephistopheles
lies in the fact that Goethe has fused the devil of the
popular German imagination with a type of dramatic
character, complementary to his own temperament,
which, in his early period, he was able to draw with
perfection, namely, that which we find exemplified
in the character of Don Carlos in *Clavigo*. But
Goethe would not have been the artist he was, had
he not possessed in a high degree the Protean power
of assuming many forms, of splitting up his own
wondrously complex personality into many simpler

component parts ; Goethe is not only Clavigo and
Faust, he is also at the same time Don Carlos and
Mephistopheles. It is well to read the *Urfaust*
before we approach the completed poem ; for it
affords a kind of æsthetic foundation, and prevents
us being carried away by the philosophic speculations which the later phases of the poem induce.

The completed First Part of *Faust*, as it appeared
in 1808, is, compared with the *Urfaust*, a veritable
patchwork ; it is full of irreconcilable contradictions,
and much more obscure in reality than the Second
Part. On to the naïve tragedy of the seventies,
Goethe has endeavoured to graft a philosophic
purpose. And as his art gradually developed from
the personal individualism of " Sturm und Drang "
to the more objective methods he acquired in Italy,
so the individual fates and sufferings of Faust gradually assumed a wider and more typical significance.
The hero changes from a man in his best years
to a brooding moralist, who requires a rejuvenat-
ing draught to make the original Gretchen tragedy
possible at all ; the sharply-drawn popular devil
of the *Urfaust* becomes a philosophically constructed
incarnation of evil, and an evil, moreover, that is
but part of a larger good. Faust's own attitude to
the devil, originally mere heroic defiance, becomes
vastly complicated by issues which extend far beyond personal responsibility and guilt. The simple

moral issue of a wrong-doing which meets with its
appointed reward, becomes a refined and complicated
problem of the balance of good and evil in the world,
the object of a wager between Heaven and Hell;
and behind it all lies a wide generalisation of the
meaning of guilt, as not a mere succumbing to
temptation, but a ceasing to strive, an inability to
rehabilitate oneself. In order to focus the old play
to the new point of view, to give universal significance to what was originally merely an individual
fate, to make Faust once more something of what
the original Faust of the sixteenth century had been,
a figure typical of the aspirations of his age,
Goethe transformed his drama into a mystery
play, or rather encapsuled the individual tragedy in
a kind of envelope, which takes the form of two Pro-
logues. The Prologue in Heaven, in particular, at
once provided the drama with a vaster background.
The problem of *Faust* becomes the problem of the
Book of Job ; Faust is now a puppet in the hands
of higher powers ; he is no longer an irresponsible
agent, free to sin and work out his own salvation,
but an object for whose possession the powers of
Heaven and Hell contend. On earth God gives this
devil, who, in accordance with that optimism,
inherited by Goethe from eighteenth - century
rationalism, cannot extricate himself from the mesh
of necessity which makes him an agent of God's

will, full power over Faust ; he may do his utmost
to lead him downwards. If Faust withstands
Mephistopheles's temptations, as God, in his Divine
foresight, knows he will, the devil loses his wager.

The problem which the poet had now to face was,
given Faust's personal fate as he had already described it, how was it to be brought into harmony
with the defeat of Mephistopheles, which the problem of the poem demanded ?   Obviously the Faust
that we already know from the earliest form of the
drama did not, in the ordinary acceptance of the
word, succeed in rising superior to the tempter.   But
Goethe saw deeper now ; he saw that the mere
yielding to the temptations of the devil is not
the real ground for the repudiation of an erring
sinner by God.   Goethe gives, however, his devil
the belief that this is so ; hence the self-confidence
of Mephistopheles who knows, when he accepts
God's wager, that he will have no difficulty in de-
vising temptations which Faust will be unable to
resist.   The Prologue in Heaven had put the matter
in another light.   Such guilt as Faust involved
himself in, or was to involve himself in, in relation
to Gretchen, was no longer to be a ground for
damnation, but only the falling away from God,
which was to manifest itself in an admission on
Faust's part that the issue of his struggle was lost.
Not the yielding to Mephistopheles's temptations,

in other words, was to constitute his guilt, but the blunting of Faust's soul by these temptations.

Thus the original tragedy of Faust, of the book-worm who, disgusted by the vanity of all knowledge, goes out into the world to be a man among men, and drink the experiences of humanity to the dregs, becomes a " divine comedy " of God's servant, a Faust in whom was embodied the best elements of eighteenth-century humanism. The new Faust is confronted by Mephistopheles, not as one who is ready to fling away the better part of life, but as a humanist, whose disenchantment has been temporary, who knows that his salvation lies in the fullest understanding of his fellow-mortals. The demands he makes on Mephistopheles, when he comes to sign the pact, are very different from those which the old Faust would have demanded, had Goethe worked out the scene at first. Mephistopheles offers himself now as Faust's servant. In the " Volksbuch," the devil undertook to do all Faust asked him for twenty-four years, and at the end of that time Faust was to fall into his hands ; but in Goethe's pact there is no limit of time, there are no concrete conditions. It would have been useless, indeed, for Mephistopheles to have dangled before the new Faust the trivial sensual joys which had entrapped the old one. For Faust has already run through the whole gamut of emotion ; from heaven-scaling jubilation to

the pessimism of despair no emotion is foreign to him ;
and the joys of the world seem to him as empty as
its sorrows—illusions one and all.   The only stipula-
tion which it is possible for Mephistopheles to make,
is that, if temptation ever succeed in drawing Faust
down, in making him forget his aspirations, in
destroying the natural elasticity of his soul, then,
and then only, he may fall a prey to the devil.   This
is the meaning of the conditions of the pact :

> If e'er upon my couch, stretched at my ease, I lie,
> Then may my life that instant cease !
> Canst thou with lying flattery rule me,
> Until, self-pleased, myself I see,—
> Canst thou with rich enjoyment fool me,
> Let that day be the last for me !
> Be this our wager. . . .
> When to the moment I shall say,
> " Linger a while !   Thou art so fair ! "
> Then mayst thou fetter me straightway,
> My final ruin then declare !

It would be impossible to defend the Second Part
of *Faust* by applying to it the same criteria of great
dramatic poetry which have been applied to the
First.   It is a shadowy, intangible poem, in which
the characters are even more indistinct than the
generalised types which people Goethe's post-
Italian creations ;   even in the case of the two
protagonists of the poem, Faust and Mephistopheles,

it is impossible to speak of continuity ; the Second
Part virtually introduces to us still another Faust,
as different from that of the poem of 1808 as the
latter was different from the Faust of Goethe's
Frankfort period ; even Mephistopheles has become
a mere pale, philosophical ghost of his former self.
But to be just to the Second Part, we must take up
a different standpoint towards it. It is not to be
treated lightly merely because it is conceived and
written according to other ideals than the First Part.
It contains verses even more wonderful, and often
more melodious ; it is instinct with great thoughts
that flash light on the dark places of human life
and destiny ; it conjures up pictures of a vast and
solemn beauty. We might have preferred a moving
drama, pulsating with the vivid life that is to be
found in the Gretchen tragedy ; we may resent the
intrusion of philosophy and allegory, and regret that
Goethe should have continued the most realistic,
actual tragedy in the world's literature as a dream-
like, intellectual phantasmagoria ; but our business
is, after all, not with the Second Part of *Faust*
as it might have been, but with the Part as it is.
If it is an allegory, we must frankly accept it
and judge it as such, not condemn it, before
we have even tried to find the key to its meaning.
Even the most cursory reader soon feels that there
is some elusive mystery behind the vapid figures

G

and incidents, which hardly awaken at all our emotional interest.

" People come to me," said Goethe once to Ecker-mann, with whom he often discussed his work on the drama, " and ask me what ideas I have tried to incorporate in my *Faust*. As if I knew myself and could say. ' From Heaven through the world to Hell ! ' that is something, if they must have some-thing ; but that is the course of the action, not an idea. Or again, we might say, that the devil loses his wager, and that a man who, amidst serious errors and aberrations, always strives upwards towards better things, is to be saved ; that again is a good and efficient thought which explains much, but it is not one which lies behind the whole and behind every scene. It would indeed have been a pretty mess had I been obliged to string, like beads on a single thread, all the varied and manifold life of *Faust*." In these words Goethe gave expression to the repugnance of the artist to reduce his work to a formula, and also to the difficulty of provid-ing a single formula which should explain a poem that had been written at widely different periods and according to very different plans. The simple moral issue of wrong-doing had, as we have seen, become a complicated problem of the balance of good and evil in the world, and the fate of the in-dividual hero was merged in an allegorical presenta-

tion of human activity and ultimate salvation of the
racial type. Goethe was never weary of telling us to
" become what we are " ; that is to say, to make
the utmost of the powers and faculties with which
we happen to be endowed, to face life with that
" holy earnestness," into which the hero of his
greatest novel was initiated at the close of his apprenticeship. This is the practical philosophy which
Goethe embodied in his poem ; Faust is saved by
virtue of his restless striving, his insatiable greed
of activity. More than this, Faust learns, in the
course of the long Second Part—an allegory of human
experience such as has never before or since been
encompassed in a single poem—to be wisely active,
to limit his practical activity to his " God-given
hest," to ends that lie within his power. In other
words, that, unquenchable as is and must be man's
striving, it can only become a great positive force
in the world if it is guided by a higher wisdom
that voluntarily recognises the limits of individual
activity.

Between the tragic close of Part I. and the open-
ing of Part II. a long period necessarily elapses,
in which Faust is lulled back to mental and emotional
equilibrium by the beneficent forces of nature.
When we see him again, it is at the Court of
the Emperor, where Mephistopheles's object is to
introduce him to a wider human activity, in which

personal ends are subordinated to social. With Mephistopheles's aid he soon becomes an indispensable person at the court ; he relieves the financial difficulties of the state by the introduction of paper money, and for the Emperor's delectation conjures up Helen of Troy. All this is embedded in a kind of masquerade which leaves us entirely cold nowadays, but which had a peculiar fascination for the German mind in the earlier years of the last century. The masquerade and the paper money interest Faust little, but the vision of the fairest woman in the world touches his emotional nature anew, although in a very different way from that in which Gretchen had attracted him. Faust has risen on his dead life to higher things ; Helen is not merely a woman who kindles in him love, but an embodiment of that ideal beauty which gives his life its higher inspiration. Mephistopheles still hopes in his blind, unseeing way that Helen may succeed where Gretchen failed, and satisfy the craving and striving whereby Faust still eludes him ; and when Faust demands the real Helen, in place of the shadow he had conjured up to amuse the Emperor, he, powerless himself to bring Helen back, points out to Faust the way that leads to the mysterious " mothers," those guardians of the eternal ideals, from whom he will receive the key that opens up the way through the centuries.

Meanwhile Mephistopheles, dissatisfied in finding
that Faust's erotic feelings have been raised,
as it were, to a higher, more spiritual plane, endeavours to distract him from his vision of Greek
beauty by means drawn from that medieval world
in which he is more at home. But even here
Mephistopheles cannot evade his fate, foreshadowed
by God in the prologue, that all his efforts to
work evil only result ultimately in good. The
" Homunculus," a tiny being, which is produced
in a retort, like a chemical product, by Faust's
famulus Wagner, only helps Faust to attain his
object ; for it is the Homunculus who, in one of
the most grotesquely imagined scenes in the whole
range of dramatic literature, leads Faust to that
vision of antique beauty, the " classical Walpurgis-
nacht." At last Faust gains his heart's desire ;
he finds his way back to classic antiquity, to the
real Helen of Troy. The third act, which was published long before the completed Second Part, is
a masterpiece of Goethe's classic art ; it is per-
vaded by that Hellenism which it was the aim of
Weimar classicism to bring back, like Helen herself,
from the antique world into the romantic medievalism
of the northern world. In fact, the *Helena* is an
allegory of the classic-romantic movement of the
time, and the wonderfully picturesque scene where
Helen and her Greek women, shrinking before the

barbaric splendour of the German middle ages, are received by Faust in his turreted castle, is an allegory of the classic Goethe's mission in poetry.

Obviously the restless, striving Faust cannot remain here ; were Helen to have satisfied him, the hour of Mephistopheles's triumph would have come. Beauty is no end in itself, and it is Helen's rôle not to satisfy him, but to lead him onwards to a wide activity in the service of humanity. Through his love for Helen, Faust passes through that " æsthetic education " which Schiller had praised as the portal to the higher life ; it was the most precious lesson which the classic literature of Germany had to teach, the education and liberation of humanity by means of the beautiful.

And in Act IV., where the allegory is most concentrated, and, it must be added, least successful, Faust is won back to a life of action, passes from the quest of an æsthetic ideal to practical life as a man among men. To Mephistopheles he appears a greater riddle than ever ; it passes beyond the devil's comprehension how any mortal, provided, as Faust had been, with all that is desirable in life, should turn his back on it and plunge into a new activity that means labour, hardship, and doubtful success. Again Faust places his services at the disposal of his Emperor, this time not to relieve financial necessity or while away an idle hour, but

for the grim business of war ; and in return, the
Emperor grants him a strip of land by the sea.
Goethe, with that fantastic love of allegory which
is the last infirmity of noble poetic minds, makes
his Faust create the very land over which he is to
rule ; he founds a new state on a strip of coast-land
which he has regained from the sea. In Act V.
Faust's dream is realised ; his unceasing activity is
crowned with complete success ; he rules over a free
people living on a land of their own creating. At
this point Goethe, as if to show that there are limits
to human perfectibility, introduces an episode in
which Faust ruthlessly dispossesses an old couple of
their home ; the poet would apparently imply that
Faust's arrogant dreams and unlimited power have
stifled in him sympathy, that " reverence for what
is beneath us " which in Goethe's spiritual thought
was an essential element in the highest reverence,
the reverence for oneself. Faust's end draws near ;
he has reached the great age of a hundred, and
Mephistopheles knows that that final struggle for
his soul cannot long be delayed. From the smoking
ashes of the home which he has destroyed, emerge,
like Eumenides, four grey women, Want and Guilt,
Care and Need. Of these, only Care can have any
hold on Faust ; his wealth and might render the
others powerless. Care alone can steal through
the keyhole of Faust's palace, and she breathes upon

his eyes and makes him blind. But physical blindness gives Faust clearer spiritual vision, more steadfast resolution to complete the great work of his life. As Mephistopheles summons his ghostly gravediggers to dig his grave, the sound of their shovels seems to him but the music of the creative labour he himself commands. Thus active, striving to the last, Faust achieves his life-work :

> Yes, to this thought I firmly cling,
> Wisdom's last fruit profoundly true :
> Freedom alone he earns as well as life,
> Who day by day must conquer them anew.
> So here, by dangers girt, youth, manhood, age,
> Shall live a vigorous life from year to year ;
> And such a throng I fain would see
> Stand on free soil among a people free.
> Then to the moment I might say :
> Linger a while, thou art so fair !
> The traces of my earthly life
> Cannot in æons pass away.—

It is in the conquering of one's life anew with every day, not in the mere heaping up of material wealth and the acquisition of power, things that are only too apt to obscure the spiritual goal, in which man's final victory lies. Even Faust's worldly position may be understood as part of the great allegory ; for Faust stands for that pedagogic ideal which was so deeply engrained in Goethe's time ; he realises the dream of the greater rationalists of the eighteenth century in Germany from Lessing to Goethe, the " perfection in humanity " of the race.

Faust sinks down, his life has come to its appointed end. Mephistopheles triumphs ; he summons his devils to his aid, but these are beaten back by the angels who scatter roses, a scene that had a peculiar fascination for Ruskin's imagination. It is the spirit, not the letter of the law that counts. The angels bear upwards the immortal part of Faust, singing as they go :

> Gerettet ist das edle Glied
> Der Geisterwelt vom Bösen :
> Wer immer strebend sich bemüht,
> Den können wir erlösen.

" He who strives in never-wearying activity can be redeemed by us," words which might be regarded as the key to Faust's life-problem. The drama closes as it had begun, as a medieval mystery ; amidst the wondrous imaginings of medieval theology, Faust is led upward and onward, by the woman-soul, now embodied in the earthly semblance of Gretchen, to the feet of the Virgin.

There is one problem connected with this closing symphony which in recent years has occupied Goethe critics much, namely, the very apt question as to whether Mephistopheles has not morally won his wager, whether he has not been unjustly cheated out of his booty by God. Faust has uttered the magic words which were to deliver him over to the devil; he has reached the stage when he has ceased to strive; and Goethe has not made it clear why the powers of good should, as is clearly the case, triumph in the end. Goethe himself anticipated this difficulty; in a conversation with Eckermann in 1831 he referred to the lines we have just quoted together with their continuation :

> Und hat an ihm die Liebe gar
> Von oben Teil genommen,
> Begegnet ihm die selige Schar
> Mit herzlichem Willkommen.

" And if love has gone out to him from above, the blessed host will meet him with affectionate welcome." " In those lines," said Goethe, " is contained the key to Faust's salvation : in Faust himself an ever higher and purer activity to the end, and the eternal Love coming to his aid from above. This is in complete harmony with our religious idea, according to which we are not saved by our own power, but by the Divine Mercy acting with it." This explanation does not, however, get rid of the difficulty ; the fact remains that, according to his last words, Faust has discovered a condition under which he is able to " bid the passing moment stay," namely, in the success of his altruistic energy. According to the strict letter of the law, Mephistopheles does triumph. It has been suggested that a new factor

has made itself felt in the situation in so far as it is
not really Mephistopheles who triumphs, but Time.
" Time," says Mephistopheles, " is the master of him
who has so powerfully withstood me." But the
admission is none the less there ; and therefore
Faust's soul—over which Time has no control—ought
to fall to the powers of evil. But here the optimist
in Goethe interposed : Faust is saved by the Divine
Mercy. It is the final conclusion of an optimism
on which, as Goethe says, rest the " foundations of our religion," or, as one might say, the
foundations of human faith in the Unseen and
Incomprehensible.

CHAPTER VIII

GOETHE'S PHILOSOPHY AND RELIGION

In no phase of Goethe's activity does he stand out more clearly as a poet than in his relations to abstract thinking. Living in the most "philosophic" age of the world's history, Goethe was himself no philosopher; and he constantly and emphatically deprecated any attempt to regard him as such. This does not mean that he took no interest in such matters; on the contrary, he was as keenly alive as any of his contemporaries to the movement of ideas; but he held himself aloof, he remained the onlooker. Or we might put it another way, and say that Goethe was a philosopher who expressed adherence to no system of philosophy; he was an eclectic in the sense in which that word was used at a later stage in the history of philosophy. He culled a little here and there, his selection being guided solely by his personal needs; but he had no faith in the elaborate efforts of metaphysicians to solve the ultimate problems of the universe. He was a sceptic who took his stand on what he himself regarded as common sense. It was enough for him to know what the problems were;

he regarded them as unapproachable mysteries.
He was convinced that there could be no finality
in human thought ; behind the last mountain ranges
he saw ever higher chains. For such a concrete,
unmetaphysical mind, the liberating tendencies in
Kant's thought, which superseded the utilitarian
rationalism of the previous age, were, no doubt,
welcome ; and Goethe especially appreciated Kant's
definition of the scope of the human intelligence ;
but he could have little sympathy for the universal
dogmatism of Hegelianism. In approaching every
phase of human thought or activity, Goethe first
set himself to distinguish between the knowable
and the unknowable, the attainable and the un-
attainable. He recognised cheerfully the limitations
of the human mind and declined to dogmatise about
what he ruled as lying beyond human ken. " Man
is not born to solve the problems of the world, but
rather to discover where the problems lie, and then
to keep within the limits of the comprehensible."

Goethe's own intellectual temperament naturally conditioned in the main his attitude to
metaphysics : but something must also be attributed
to the fact that in the most impressionable period
of his life he fell under the spell of Spinoza. He
had been bathed, so to speak, invulnerable in the
pantheism of Spinozism. For, if we may judge
by Goethe's case, it is the peculiarity of Spinoza's

philosophy that it does not make a man a Spinozist, as Hegel converted his adherents into Hegelians ; it rather acts as a kind of vaccine, which renders its followers immune against metaphysic dogmatism. Such, at least, was its effect on Goethe. For him Spinozism was something similar to what the Roman Catholic Church was to the early Romanticists : a source of satisfying belief that precluded the need of reopening metaphysical problems. Goethe might thus be described as a Spinozist who was indifferent to the dogmas of Spinoza ; he accepted the oneness of God with nature, but resolutely declined to question farther. This type of mind, uninquiring where the suprasensual was concerned, is by no means to be regarded as an unqualified advantage ; it no doubt made Goethe a less deep and less conclusive thinker in abstract things than Schiller ; it robbed his speculations in natural science of qualities which would have greatly enhanced their value. But in all that pertained to Goethe the artist, it was only in his favour.

Although Goethe thus took no active part in the evolution of metaphysical thinking in Germany between Kant and Hegel, he had much to say of the highest value in the field of ethical philosophy. Here, indeed, the poet's repugnance to vague speculation, his antipathy to dogmatic systems and would-be finality, stood him in excellent stead. He became the spokesman of an ethical philosophy which, in saneness and healthy common sense, excelled, as it has outlived, the ethic systems of the philosophers of his day. For Goethe succeeded in avoiding the shallow materialism of Rationalism as well as the ecstatic unbalance of the Romanticism that superseded it ; he set up a golden mean in which the very best practical thinking of the eighteenth and early nineteenth centuries is concentrated. Here Goethe still speaks to us with a living voice. When we consider Goethe as a philosopher, we thus think, not of his metaphysics, but of his ethics. None of the great poets of the world has expressed so clearly and definitely his conception of the duty of man, as Goethe has throughout the length and breadth of his works.

Perhaps the most concentrated expression of Goethe's moral philosophy is to be found—veiled, it is true, in an obscuring Leibnizian phraseology— in his aphorism *Das Höchste* : " The highest we have received from God is life, the rotating movement of the monad round itself, which knows no rest ; the impulse to maintain and cherish life is inborn and indestructible in each of us ; its peculiar nature remains, however, a secret from ourselves and others. The second favour we have received from above is experience, perception, the power of the living monad to act on its surroundings in the outside world, whereby it becomes conscious of its inward unlimitedness, and its outward limitations. . . . A third favour is the development of that activity which we direct against the outside world in the form of action, word and writing." The first duty of man, as Goethe conceived it, is to recognise frankly his limitations; to deliminate his sphere, to realise what the demands are that life makes on him. The highest practical wisdom to which Faust attains is :

> Earth's narrow sphere is known enough to me.
> The view beyond is barred from mortal sight :
> Fool ! who would yonder turn his blinking eyes
> And dream to find his like above the clouds !
> Firm let him stand and look around him here ;
> To men of worth this world is never mute.

Everyone has his appointed task to do in the world, and it is his first business to make himself clear as to what that task is. This clearness attained, it becomes his duty to act. Action is the final solution to all problems of the practical life : for " in every situation of life a definite activity is demanded of us."

When, however, we come to ask : What is the nature of this task which is imposed upon us ? how are we to recognise our peculiar duty when it presents itself to us ? Goethe is a less sure guide. It is not merely that here the great exception has a difficulty in prescribing for the ruck of mankind, but also that there was a certain duality in Goethe's ethical philosophy, two opposing and contradicting principles, which he never quite succeeded in reconciling. The first of these is his insistence that every man must develop to the full his own character and individuality. This, one might say, was the alpha and omega of Goethe's faith in his days of " Storm and Stress " ; and he repeated it again and again in varying forms in later life. There was, indeed, no conviction to which he remained more constant all his life than that the highest aim of every human life should be to develop itself to its utmost capacity. But Goethe's views underwent a change with respect to what constituted this development. The ruthlessness of his early thought soon gave place to a more temperate and deliberate conception of moral development, which in later years made it increasingly difficult for him to maintain his old individualism. In his last and ripest period his conception of the highest form of human activity and development of human personality had nothing in it of base self-aggrandisement, or of ruthless egotism ; it was an activity and a development in harmony with the interests of the social body. In Goethe's ethical philosophy, all personal desires must be restrained and subordinated to higher ends : self-sacrifice for an unselfish ideal is all-essential to the right develop-

H

ment of character. An element in all true education is " Entsagung " or renunciation, which word
assuredly did not mean self-torturing to Goethe;
he did not confuse it, as Carlyle did, with the
" Entbehren sollst du, sollst entbehren ! " of *Faust*,
or the " bitter tears " of *Wilhelm Meisters Lehrjahr*.
That was quite another matter. The " Entsagung "
of the *Wanderjahre* means only the rational ordering
of one's life, the foresight which is inherent in all
true education. We must " renounce " certain
things, not do them or enjoy them, in no spirit of
disappointment, but cheerfully, in order that we
may the more surely attain our end at a later
time. To " renounce " meant to Goethe merely to
subordinate individual desires and actions to the
interests of the whole. " Entsagung " is, as we
have ultimately to realise, for our good. It is just
this resignation of the passing happiness that
makes us free, a thought in which one seems to
catch an echo of the Kantian ethics. The victory
over self, " Selbstüberwindung," is a great positive
idea, no ascetic denial of happiness :

> Von der Gewalt, die alle Wesen bindet,
> Befreit der Mensch sich, der sich überwindet.

Goethe, then, in his outlook on the individual
life, is far from being a pessimist ; and it is not
surprising that he has been hailed by the most ad-

vanced movement of ethic philosophy on the continent as a pioneer of that " Lebensbejahung " with which Nietzsche confronted the solid phalanx of nineteenth-century pessimism since Schopenhauer. But at no stage could Goethe's optimism be described as militant or aggressive ; it, too, had " overcome itself " ; had been schooled, as Nietzsche's in our own time, in pessimism or, at least, in the eighteenth-century equivalent of pessimism. Indeed, so firmly was Goethe convinced of the harmony and rightness of God's world, that he accepted calmly all that life brought with it in a spirit not far removed from fatalism. In later years the little word " abwarten " played a great part in the poet's contemplation of life. He was a fatalist, but, paradoxical as it may seem, an optimistic fatalist :

> Nach ewigen ehrenen
> Grossen Gesetzen,
> Müssen wir alle
> Unseres Daseins Kreise vollenden.

The development of personality must, it was clear, proceed on moral lines, that is to say, be guided by certain eternal principles of right and wrong. Goethe has no answer to give us when we ask what these principles are, and how do we arrive at them ; it was not his way, as we have seen, to try to pierce behind the veil ; he leaves the ideas of right and wrong unjustified, regards them as something im-

planted in our conscience and not to be questioned.
It is, however, obvious that the right and wrong
of human action is a social conception, the
result of an evolution of social ideals ; and from
whatever point of view we look at the problem, it
introduces an altruistic element into individual
morality.

Altruism was a conspicuous feature of Goethe's
ethics, as it was of every eighteenth-century philosophy ; and it stands in constant, if not always
conscious, conflict with the principle of individualism
from which Goethe set out. He insisted, and with
ever-increasing emphasis as life went on, that the
highest activity of man must necessarily be altruistic
in character. This is embodied in the close of
Faust ; Faust discovers that his ultimate mission lies
in working for his fellow-men. The fact remains,
however, that Goethe never fairly faced the conflict
between the two principles ; in his optimistic way
he believed that, somehow or other, the individualist
and the altruist would discover a *modus vivendi*
without serious sacrifice on either side. The recon-
ciliation of these ideas was one of the problems
Goethe put aside as insoluble ; but this did not
lessen the validity of his practical philosophy. No
thinker or poet of modern times has expressed a
higher wisdom on the conduct of the individual
life than Goethe has done ; none has interpreted,

with a nearer approach to finality, that law of
conduct which Matthew Arnold used to tell us was
three-fourths of life: to take life seriously; to
do the duty that lies nearest to us; to act, not
dream, or speculate or talk; to seek salvation in
constant striving and fighting. " Ein Mensch sein
heisst ein Kämpfer sein." " Wer immer strebend
sich bemüht, den können wir erlösen." In aphor-
isms like these, Goethe has concentrated a philosophy
of conduct which is as convincing to-day as it was
in Goethe's own age.

Goethe's social philosophy has not, it must be confessed, the same firm, assured outlines and the same
present-day value, as his personal philosophy; but
when we remember the age in which Goethe lived,
this is hardly surprising. His life extended over
what, in social development, was the most momentous era in modern Europe, the era of the French
Revolution. The Revolution had much to do with
Goethe's change of front; and the Revolution was
followed by the rise of Napoleon, which again gave
Goethe much to think of concerning the relations of
the individual to the social body. Before these events
Goethe had had no occasion to revise or even seriously
consider the views on social questions which he
had accepted, as a matter of course, throughout
the years of his political activity as Minister of
State of the Duchy of Weimar. In fact, before the

French Revolution, political thinking in the modern
sense of the word had not seriously busied Goethe,
or, for that part, the entire German people, at all.
Under the *ancien régime* the existing political in-
stitutions were accepted as a time-honoured and
firmly-established arrangement of Providence in a
well-ordered world.

Thus in Weimar Goethe seconded the fatherly
absolutism of his Duke. As for practical politics,
he brushed them aside with the dogma that every
man must " sweep before his own door," that he
must be active to the best of his ability in the circle
of life in which he happened to be placed. He
never definitely formulated his pre-Revolutionary
views on these matters, but had he done so, he
would probably have said that the state was a
means to an end, that end being to obtain free
play for the development of its individual members.
He would, no doubt, have recognised that the state
often ran counter to such ideals ; but it was the
object of the " enlightened " state, such as he
helped to realise in Weimar, to interfere as little
as possible with the individual, and to make the
minimum claim on him. A natural corollary to
such a view of the state was that, political respon-
sibilities being reduced to a minimum, patriotism
was an unnecessary and superfluous sentiment,
a view which was entirely in accordance with the

cosmopolitanism of the German people in the later eighteenth century.

But first the Revolution, then Napoleon, shattered this political indifferentism. The Revolution demonstrated the futility of the eighteenth-century State to fulfil its function in anything but fair weather ; Napoleon's career showed how the colourless ideal of Weimar might at any moment be at the mercy of the individual aggressor. The common conclusion to be drawn from both phenomena was that the staying power of the State would have to be increased, if it were to resist and counteract such disintegrating forces. It is interesting to watch, as a commentary on Goethe's political thought, the reflection in his mind of the events in France. Like all the great Germans of his time, Goethe greeted the Revolution with enthusiasm, only to turn from it, as it progressed, with dismay and abhorrence ; what at first promised to be an emancipation of society from intolerable fetters, ultimately appeared to him as a triumph of brutality and darkness over the humane enlightenment which the eighteenth century regarded as its most precious achievement ; and this attitude remained tolerably constant. It lies, for instance, behind the somewhat trivial comedy *Der Bürgergeneral*, written in 1793 ; it throws a reflected light on *Hermann und Dorothea* in 1798, and it inspired *Die natürliche Tochter* in

1804. His standpoint towards Napoleon passed through more varied phases. In the beginning of his meteoric career Napoleon awakened Goethe's admiration, and even enthusiasm ; but as his power grew and spread, a certain distrust found its way into Goethe's mind, and a veritable antipathy to this man, who played fast and loose with the rights of the individual, and endangered, by his mere caprice, the validity and power of states. Later, when Napoleon's dreams had become a reality and the continent lay at his feet, Goethe's fatalism began to assert itself anew : he wondered if the success of this great, strong man had not something God-appointed in it, and his personal contact with him in the famous interview of Erfurt, when Napoleon flattered the " author of Werther " with the words " Vous êtes un homme ! " deepened his personal respect for him. So convinced did he become of Napoleon's " mission " in Europe, that he viewed with scepticism the efforts of German patriots to throw off the yoke of the oppressor. Even after the disastrous Russian campaign, Goethe maintained his faith in Napoleon. " Rattle at your chains," he said to the young poets of the War of Liberation, " the man is too great for you, you cannot break them ! " And in his own mind he justified Napoleon in Germany as a champion of culture and enlighten-ment, of that inner freedom which he prized above

independence and patriotism, as a bulwark against
the possible invasion and subjugation of Germany
by the Slavs. But again Goethe had to change his
opinion; and he did it frankly and openly. *Des
Epimenides Erwachen* (1814) echoes the patriotic
jubilation that followed the victory of Leipzig.

The change which came over Goethe's ideas of
the relation of the individual to the State in the
epoch that succeeded the Revolution meant naturally
a complete break with the old political *régime*. The
social conditions of Europe had been changed by
the Revolution and by the natural evolution of
human thought and activity in the early nineteenth
century; and Goethe had to become reconciled
to the new conditions. This, we might say, he did,
or tried to do, in *Wilhelm Meisters Wanderjahre*.
We have already seen how, on its artistic side, that
book was a profound disappointment to those who
had hoped for a real continuation of the *Lehrjahre*;
it is an even greater disappointment as an exposition
of social philosophy. Nothing, indeed, could show
more clearly how difficult it was for Goethe, a
denizen of the eighteenth century, to arrive at clear
ideas about the new social and political developments of the nineteenth. In the *Wanderjahre*
he has honestly tried to adopt a new standpoint; he
frankly realised that the rise of industrialism, and
the development of machinery, had created entirely

new conditions ; that the increased potency of
human activity, and the correspondingly rapid
accumulation of wealth, demanded a revised theory
of the body social and politic. But he finds the
new era overwhelming in its complexity, and in
face of that complexity he virtually fell back—
just as in metaphysics he had given himself over to
Spinoza—on the old " contrat social " of Rousseau.
Thus Goethe, the most individualistic of poets,
becomes in his old age an exponent of uncompromising socialism. The State is no longer to exist to
foster the individual ; individuals only exist to
constitute the State.

But one must at least give Goethe credit for a
certain reluctance in enunciating these views ;
he regarded this State socialism as a kind of *pis
aller* ; it was not so much his own personal ideal
as what seemed to him the goal towards which the
world was moving. In other words, Goethe was
nonplussed ; he could not understand the development of the world, and he let his old individualistic
faith go. He was no more able to discover the
germs of a new individualism in the Romantic
thought of the early nineteenth century than he
was able to foresee the great poetic forces that were
ultimately to rise from the ashes of pessimism.

It was but natural that the unwillingness which
Goethe showed to tie himself down to dogmatic

systems in philosophy should have manifested itself in his religious thought. One remembers the elusiveness of Faust's confession about his religion to Gretchen, a passage which dates from Goethe's days of " Sturm und Drang " ; and all his life long Goethe was equally unwilling to formulate his own religious beliefs. Religion, the relation of the soul to God, was to him—imbued as he had been in early life with the spiritual shyness of pietism— a Holy of Holies into which he refused to allow the outsider to pry. To Goethe, the Spinozist, religion was an all-pervading thing that imbued man's whole life and activity ; and it was as possible for it to manifest itself in art and literature as in the special attitude of the mind to faith and doctrine.

> Wer Wissenschaft und Kunst besitzt,
> Hat auch Religion ;
> Wer jene beiden nicht besitzt,
> Der habe Religion.

> ("He who possesses learning and art, has also religion ;
> let him who has not these things have religion.")

He told Jacobi once that as a poet and an artist he was a polytheist, as a scientist a pantheist, the one as decidedly as the other. " If I require a god for my personality as a moral being, one has also been provided."

The pulse of Goethe's religious sentiment is obviously not to be sought in any adherence to

sectarian dogmas, but rather in that attitude of mind
which we have already found manifested in his
metaphysic and moral theorising, namely, the frank
recognition of man's limitations and the equally
frank recognition of the existence of mysteries and
problems beyond our ken. What to him made
the religious nature was just this sense of limitation, this belief in powers, working for our good,
which transcend our intelligence. Perhaps the
nearest approach to an enunciation of Goethe's
religious faith is to be found in those wonderful
pages of the *Wanderjahre*, which explain the doctrine
of the Three Reverences :

" Three kinds of gestures you have seen : and
we inculcate a threefold reverence, which, when
commingled and formed into one whole, attains
its highest force and effect. The first is, reverence for what is above us. . . . Then comes
the second, reverence for what is under us. . . .
But from this we delay not to free our pupil the
instant we become convinced that the instruction
connected with it has produced sufficient influence
on him. Then, on the contrary, we bid him gather
courage, and, turning to his comrades, range
himself along with them. Now, at last, he stands
forth, frank and bold, not selfishly isolated :
only in combination with his equals does he front
the world. Further we have nothing to add. . . .
The religion which depends on reverence for what

is above us we denominate the ethnic ; it is the religion of the nations and the first happy deliverance from a degrading fear : all heathen religions, as we call them, are of this sort, whatsoever names they may bear. The second religion, which founds itself on reverence for what is around us, we denominate the philosophical ; for the philosopher stations himself in the middle, and must draw down to him all that is higher, and up to him all that is lower : and only in this medium condition does he merit the title of Wise. . . . The third religion, grounded on reverence for what is beneath us, we name the Christian, as in the Christian such a temper is with most distinctness manifested : it is a last step to which mankind were fitted and destined to attain."

" To which of these religions do you specially adhere ? " inquired Wilhelm.

" To all the three," replied they ; " for in their union they produce what may properly be called the true religion. Out of those three reverences springs the highest reverence—reverence for one's self ; and those again unfold themselves from this : so that man attains the highest elevation of which he is capable, that of being justified in reckoning himself the best that God and Nature have produced—nay, of being able to continue on this lofty eminence, without being again, by self-conceit and presumption, drawn down from it into the vulgar level."

Such a doctrine, cabalistically expressed as it

is here, is the last link in the development of
eighteenth-century religious enlightenment. The
narrow-sighted deism of the early time, combined
with the materialistic sacrifice of faith to morality,
which was inherent in the Rationalism of the middle
of the eighteenth century, widened and deepened in
Goethe's mind to a spiritual conception of the universe as God's and a reverence for the created
world, suffused by an unswerving optimism.

Goethe's nature was, no doubt, an intensely religious one, not in any doctrinaire, or even Christian
sense. But his belief in the right governance of the
universe was unassailable; his reliance and faith
in God was the corner-stone of his optimism; it,
too, was the basis for that intense personal fatalism
which, as we have seen, coloured all his activity;
and it inspired his Olympic tranquillity of outlook
in later years. Religious, too, was that reverence
with which he regarded the gift so generously
bestowed on himself, the gift of genius. The unconscious, mysterious thing called inspiration was
to him a veritable gift of God; and his favourite
word for describing it—whether in himself or in a
Napoleon—" dæmonic," was a tacit acknowledg-
ment of the guiding hand of a Higher Power.
" Every productivity of the highest kind, every
significant aperçu, every invention, every great
thought, which bears fruit and leads to other

thoughts, stands outside our control and is raised high above all earthly powers. Man has to regard such things as unhoped-for gifts from above. . . . In such cases, he is often to be looked upon as the tool of the higher world-government, as a vessel that has been found worthy for the reception of a divine influence."

CHAPTER IX

GOETHE AS A SCIENTIST AND CRITIC

GOETHE, one might say, was the last of those poly-historic, Aristotelian geniuses who have been able to span with equal, unflagging enthusiasm all fields of human activity. No man whose main business in life was poetry, has ever manifested so whole-hearted an interest in natural science, in art, and in politics as Goethe. There is, however, on the part of his critics an excusable tendency to regard Goethe with leniency in respect of these multiform interests ; to take seriously what in lesser mortals would be summarily dismissed as the merest dilet-tantism. Goethe's self-judgment was, no doubt, not always correct : he had—unfortunately, when we remember the claims it made on his time—an unreasonably high opinion of his talents in the fine arts ; and he had also a higher opinion of his im-portance as a man of science than was justified by his achievements. And it is just in this field that he has been treated with what appears to be excessive indulgence.

There can be no question of the seriousness of Goethe's interest in the natural sciences ; they

formed the solid foundation for all his speculation, and his occupation with them was throughout his life more persistent than was that with
poetry. Goethe's method of approaching such
sciences as biology, optics and geology seems,
however, strangely in antagonism with his methods
in other fields. Goethe's intellectual life was
governed, as we have just seen, by a healthy principle of *a posteriori* reasoning; he progressed from
fact to theory, a point that is nowhere more clearly
brought out than in his correspondence and relations with Schiller, whose intellectual methods were
purely *a priori*. But Goethe did not enter upon his
most important scientific work in this spirit, not as
the humble, unbiassed investigator, but as the theorist
who wished to see his theories substantiated. He
may himself have believed that he was subordinating
the hypothesis to the fact, using it merely as a
scaffolding, and he has, no doubt, many wise things
to say about observation and experiment being the
only true bases of science ; but the spirit of the time
was too strong for him ; and in the incubating
period of modern science the hypothesis played,
and rightly played, a great rôle. Goethe thus really
approached science as the intuitive philosopher,
and as the poet.

In biology, where his work has most significance,
he was led to the problems by that holy reverence

I

for Nature, which had been instilled in him in
early days by Rousseau and Rousseau's German
apostles : he was inspired by the great idea of
spiritual evolution, which, first dimly outlined by
Vico, was expressed with suggestive force by Herder ;
and he applied the ideas of Herder, who was
anything but a scientist, to the world of Nature,
which Rousseau had taught him to love. This
Nature was no mere collection of blind happenings,
but one and indivisible, a manifestation of God,
His "living garment," an organically developing
phenomenon. Goethe sought continuity everywhere ; and in his quest of continuity he lighted on
two widely significant discoveries—both really arrived
at by *a priori* methods—the existence of a rudi-
mentary intermaxillary bone in man, and what he
called the "metamorphosis of plants," that is to
say, the theory according to which the organs of a
plant are all modifications of the leaf.

The success of these investigations was a little
unfortunate, for it led Goethe to view his achievements with excessive self-confidence. He had made
these discoveries alone and unaided ; he was
proud of them, and this pride engendered an over-
bearing sense of superiority to the other scientific
workers of his time. Consequently he came into
no kind of touch with these, but only with philosophical scientists, like his friends in Jena, who were

influenced by the metaphysical theories of Fichte and Schelling. This was naturally calculated to increase rather than counteract the *a priori* method with which he had set out. Had Goethe, in these years when he was most exclusively interested in science, worked in hearty co-operation with the French and English representatives of empiric scientific thinking and investigation, it would have prevented him falling into the errors of his geological theories and his almost childish unwillingness to let the abstruseness of mathematics—one science to which his polyhistoric interest did not extend—come between him and the phenomena of light and colour.

As a scientific writer Goethe made his debut in 1784 with his paper on the intermaxillary bone ; and in 1790 appeared his book on the *Metamorphosis of Plants*. The investigations which resulted in the latter treatise were undertaken in the first instance as a protest against the artificialities of the Linnean system. Linné had reduced the plant-world to a mosaic wanting in any organic ground-plan or binding-principles. Goethe, starting from his preconceived view of Nature as a harmonious whole, endeavoured to establish unity in the vegetable world ; he conceived a kind of ideal " Urpflanze," from which theoretically all plants could be deduced. Branch, calyx, petal, stamen, fruit, were so many different modifications of the simple leaf. This

theory was doubtless an enormous step forward in
the direction of evolutional biology ; and it was
but a transference of it to the animal world when
he applied a similar line of reasoning to the skeleton
of mammals in his *Entwurf einer Einleitung in die
vergleichende Anatomie* (1795). In place of the
typical, symbolical plant, Goethe here saw the
animal centred in the vertebral column, which throws
out appendages, just as the stem throws out leaves ;
and, as at its highest point the stem bears flower
and fruit, so the six uppermost vertebræ develop
to form the crowning organ of the animal, its head.

It is not to be denied that in these morphological
studies Goethe had at least a glimpse of that theory
of organic evolution which Darwin was to establish
a generation and more later. An aphorism like the
following clearly foreshadows Darwinism : " Nature
can attain to anything she sets out to achieve only
by means of a gradual succession. She makes no
leaps. She could not, for example, make a horse,
if it had not been preceded by all the other animals,
as a kind of ladder by which she ascended to the
structure of the horse." Or again : " Nature, in
order to arrive at man, institutes a long prelude of
beings and forms which are, it is true, deficient in
a great deal that is essential to man. But in each is
visible a tendency which points to the next form
above it." There is, however, a very material distinc-

tion between the reasoning that expresses itself in
such a form and Darwinism. Goethe and Darwin
approached the same problem from opposite sides.
Goethe's conception of evolution was not based,
like that of the English pioneers of the theory,
on a synthesis of scientific investigations, but was
rather a deduction from a theory. It was a mere
corollary to his conception of the universe as a
harmonious whole. The ideas went back through
Herder to the old Leibnizian " Theodicée," which
put its stamp on the whole eighteenth century.
Nature was not and could not be an enemy of man,
" red in tooth and claw," as she appeared to an
analytic, scientific age, but rather a great harmonious
entity, into which it was man's highest privilege
and happiness to fit himself.

Thus although modern biology has arrived at
conclusions towards which Goethe's speculations
pointed, and although the modern scientist feels
in sympathy with him and may even, like Haeckel,
look to him as a pioneer of the theory of organic
evolution, the fact remains that Goethe was not,
and could not have been, a scientist of the modern
type ; he arrived at his results by mental processes
which modern science has discarded. He built up
his ideas on a pantheistic philosophy and a fatalistic
belief in the goodness of the universe ; he saw
in evolution the expression in Nature, of the gradu-

ally unfolding mind of God, working in the "loom of time"; whatever Goethe was, he was not, as he is often represented to be, a purely deductive thinker, with no thought for anything but the record of observation and experiment, no belief that went beyond the concrete.

The best proof that Goethe did not mean by evolution what Darwin meant, is to be seen in his blindness to the ultimate significance of the evolutional theory for the natural sciences. Science in Goethe's day had, in fact, not yet progressed far enough on empiric lines to be able to avail itself of such a theory. The chief obstacle in his way lay in the fact that he was, as we have seen in the preceding chapter, limited by strict boundaries of the knowable and unknowable; the principle of arbitrary limitation, however healthy in the regulating of human conduct, is a serious bar to the furthering of science; here the mind which dogmatises as to which problems are soluble and which are not, is lost. Thus, just as Goethe had little patience with psychological investigation, and only approved in a half-hearted way, or not at all, the preoccupation of his contemporaries with metaphysics, so he was prevented by his preconceived conclusions from giving his theory of organic development the wider application of which it was capable. There was clearly no room for an *Origin of Species* in an investigator who could say : " When the earth had arrived at a certain point of maturity . . . mankind arose everywhere where the soil permitted of it . . . to reflect on this, as has been done, I hold to be a useless occupation which we may leave to those who are fond of busying themselves with insoluble problems."

With Goethe's other scientific writings we need not take up much space ; the zeal with which he prosecuted the study of geology is born witness to by the fact that it overflowed into the Second Part of *Faust*. The geological world of those days was divided into two opposing camps, Vulcanists, who maintained that the earth's crust was the product of igneous action, and Neptunists, who maintained the aqueous origin of the globe. Goethe belonged to the latter class, and again, on purely *a priori* grounds ; his adherence to this theory did not imply that he had reviewed and weighed the evidence, but merely that he could believe in no Nature who proceeded with her work spasmodically or violently. Vulcanism implied cataclysms, and cataclysms were contrary to the smooth and harmonious working of the universe. That was all. Goethe's investigations into the science of optics, and more particularly the theory of colour, bulk largely among his scientific works. His history of the theory of colour is admirably written, and in the patient investigation and experimentation with colour, Goethe has approached more nearly than in his biological work to what we should nowadays regard as the proper attitude and method of the man of science towards his facts. But unfortunately his work in this province is marred by a quite unreasonable and unscientific antagonism to the Newtonian theory of light. Not that Goethe is necessarily wrong—among his defenders was a no less distinguished thinker than Schopenhauer—and Newton necessarily right; but before anyone has a right to proclaim an opponent wrong, he must follow him into all the intricacies of his proof. This Goethe did not, and—owing to his small mathematics—could not do; and so virtually on the basis of his own inaptitude for that science, he pronounced the mathematical investigation of the theory of light wrong.

In his critical appreciation of literature and art, Goethe was tinged with the universalism and cosmopolitanism of his epoch. In his youth, in those militant criticisms of the *Frankfurter gelehrte Anzeigen* and elsewhere, he defended the ideas of the " Sturm und Drang " as formulated by men like Herder and Gerstenberg : the contempt for the rules, the rights of genius, and revolt against authority. In later life he turned with understanding to the products of a classic and even a pseudo-classic art. The Goethe who in his youth had overflowed in boundless enthusiasm for Shakespeare, translated in middle life the *Mahomet* and *Tancrède* of Voltaire for the Weimar stage, and pruned and purified, in approved Gallic fashion, the *Romeo and Juliet* of Shakespeare. But Goethe's later developments never entirely obscured his earlier judgments; the old principles remained even where a personal antipathy was involved. Thus we find him in later years speaking with admirable clearness and fairness of the writings of the Romantic School, and that at a time when he had but little sympathy for that school's tendencies. The few cases where Goethe's judgment played him false—in the case of Kleist, for example—are so exceptional that they only bring home to us anew how reliable his opinion in literature was. One antipathy, however, he brought with him from earlier years, an antipathy he could never overcome, namely, to the Middle Ages. The Middle Ages meant nothing to him personally; at most he could speak with a certain understanding and national pride, if without enthusiasm, of the *Nibelungenlied*; but the intellectual darkness, the lack of any sense of style, above all, the grotesque and tyrannous forms of medieval religious thought, were abhorrent to him; and in his eyes Dante, the one great "world-poet" whose poetry could make no personal appeal to him, was still a medieval poet.

To one literature only did his allegiance never
waver, the literature of Greece. Here he was the
true heir of the century of humanitarianism. In
Greece he found the fullest and most serene expression of the " Allgemeinmenschliche " to which it is
the highest problem of art and poetry to give visible
form. Shakespeare came and went in his affections,
but in his allegiance to Homer he remained constant
all his life long, from those early days of *Werthers
Leiden*, when the pictures of Homer's world, as
the ideal of spiritual health, were obscured, as his
hero loses his mental tranquillity and balance, by
the romantic mists of Ossian. Homer was his
ideal in his classical period ; and the next place
in his affections belonged to the Greek tragic poets,
above all, to Sophocles. Goethe was in the fullest
sense of that often abused term a Hellenist ; but
his Hellenism never came into conflict with anti-
Hellenism, at least not as it did in Heine's case.
The antique world remained for him the most
human and humane expression of man's aspirations ;
time and again he insisted on the need of all true
culture being based on that of Greece, and on the
ancient tongues being the indispensable basis of all
true education.

But, on the whole, there is comparatively little
literary criticism in Goethe's works ; he has written
less, in a systematic way, about literature or its

history than any other of the greater German poets. On the other hand, many volumes of his works are filled with his opinions on art. But here his views were distinctly narrower, partly because he had gone through no phases in art corresponding to the "Sturm und Drang" unrest in literature ; the enthusiasm for Gothic architecture in Strassburg, which in later life he repudiated, was never really incompatible with his classic tastes. Consequently the classicism of Winkelmann passed on in Goethe's mind unbroken into the classicism which he maintained in his own book on Winkelmann, in his *Propyläen* and in *Über Kunst und Altertum*. Goethe was a far less tolerant Hellenist in art than in literature. The plastic masterpieces of Greece, especially the Elgin Marbles, were to him the last word in artistic expression ; and, as we have seen, when he went to Italy he followed virtually in the footsteps of Winkelmann. He had no eyes for anything but the antique ; and Renaissance art only appealed to him in so far as it strove after classic imitation and classic excellence, a point of view which necessarily, and in spite of much genuine admiration, led him to a quite false view of artists like Michel Angelo and Leonardo da Vinci. Only in the case of Raphael does he seem disposed to make an exception. Raphael is not a "classic," but he stands on the heights of genius, and before such genius, before such a "re-born Greek," criticism must be dumb. Such being Goethe's standpoint, one need have little surprise that the beginnings of a new Romantic art in the early nineteenth century were abhorrent to him, and for the romantic "Nazarenertum" that sprang from the religious ecstasies of the first Romantic School, as for the literary expression of that attitude of mind, books like Wackenroder's *Herzensergiessungen*, he was never weary of expressing his dislike.

CHAPTER X

GOETHE'S PERSONALITY ; CONCLUSION

WHEN all has been said that can be said about Goethe's magnificent activity, we ultimately come back to the proposition with which we set out : Goethe's supreme work is himself. What Friedrich Schlegel said of Lessing might with more justice be said of Goethe : " He himself was of more worth than all his talents ; in his individuality lay his greatness." The key to his works is his personality ; he was the most " personal " of poets and the greatest personality among poets. His entire literary activity was in quite a unique degree the reflection of that personality. Again and again he explained—as if this were in the least necessary, or, indeed, anything but obvious—that his own writings were all subjective, even " occasional." The clearest confession on this matter is perhaps to be found in an often quoted passage from his autobiography : " If I desired for my poems a basis of truth, a feeling or reflection, I had to turn to my own heart ; if I required for my poetic representation an immediate intuition of an object or event, I could not go beyond the circle which was capable of appealing to me, of inspiring me with an interest. In this way I first wrote certain little poems in the form of songs, or in a freer measure ; they are founded on reflection, treat of the past and, for the most part, take an epigrammatic turn. And so began that tendency with which, all my life long, I was unable to break, namely, that of turning into an image, into a poem, whatever delighted or pained me, or otherwise occupied me, and of coming to a conclusion with myself about it, that I might both rectify my ideas of outward things and set my mind at rest about them. The faculty of being able to do this was, no doubt, to no one more necessary than it was to me, for my nature was always throwing me from one extreme to the other. Thus everything that I have put into writing is only a fragment of a great confession."

At the same time—as we have already seen in considering the works of Goethe's middle period—there is a very real danger of carrying the genetic method of interpretating Goethe's works too far ; in other words, seeking everywhere for the confession, discovering models for characters, actual experiences behind scenes and situations, even "explaining" on a subjective basis the most intangible lyric gems. The temptation to employ such a method does not merely arise from Goethe's own insistence on the personal element in his work,

but in the fact that we are more richly provided
in the case of Goethe than of any other poet with
the materials for carrying out such a method.   It
might even be argued that Goethe's works are,
after all, no more personal and subjective than
those of other great poets who were not too burdened
with literary conventions ;   only in their case we
are freer to judge by purely impersonal canons,
because the means of judging otherwise are denied
to us.

We cannot attempt in this brief concluding chapter
to sum up that magnificent personality which lies
unfolded in Goethe's published writings.   The most
striking feature in it—the feature that stamps
Goethe as the great exception—is its universality
and balance ;   that quality which led Carlyle to see
in Goethe the exemplar of the wise man.   Goethe
was sane and healthy, as few of the great men of
our race are, whose strength lies in their imagination,
whose mode of expression is art.   He was a " Lebens-
künstler " in the great style, and he succeeded,
beyond his highest dreams, in rearing that pyramid
of his life which in early life he had so nobly planned.
An earlier generation was much troubled about what
they called Goethe's ruthless egotism ;   he was
described as the " apostle of self-culture," behind
which lay a reproach similar to that which was
implied in the phrase " the great Heathen," which

our Victorian moralists used to apply to him. But one hears little nowadays of Goethe's "heathenism," and in our modern age the abnegation of self-culture, of the fullest development of all our faculties, would be regarded in a different light.

The balance and sanity of Goethe's nature is to be seen in the conduct of his own life. It was a peculiarly difficult life to conduct, for Goethe was endowed in a superlative degree with the artist's sensitiveness to impressions ; he had a temperament peculiarly exposed to great enthusiasms ; it was the kind of life which—as we see in only too many of the German poets and artists— without a firm, guiding character would have gone off at a tangent, have been unbalanced by dissipation. And, on the whole, it was a happy life. We say this not unmindful of that confession which Goethe made to Eckermann a few years before his death : " I have always been praised as one who was especially favoured by fortune ; nor will I complain. . . . But at bottom it has been nothing but toil and trouble, and I think I may say that in all my seventy-five years I have never known four weeks of real well-being." That Goethe suffered keenly, that he learned bitter lessons in " nights spent in tears," is true, as it is true of all who are keenly sensitive to the world around them ; but that he passed through

a period of romantic renunciation, as Novalis, and
after him, Carlyle, would have had us think, was
not the case.   There was no tinge of resigning pessimism in Goethe's nature ; he was essentially
buoyant, optimistic. He suffered, as he enjoyed, with
great intensity ; but he was always capable, so to
speak, of detaching himself, of regarding his suffering as a mere onlooker at himself. Even in the
most intense moments of despair he could see
himself as an artist might look at a model
in whom he had no personal interest.   Never,
even in his darkest moments, when he dallied
with thoughts of suicide, did his own personality
stand in danger of disintegration ; he was himself
no Werther.

Looking back once more on Goethe's extraordinarily varied literary output, we might ask :
In what form of poetry did Goethe most excel ?
where is he to be found at his best and highest ?
Most critics will no doubt answer, in the lyric.   In
the epic he did not get beyond the idyll, or, if we
will include his prose fiction under the heading
epic, novels like *Werther* or *Meister*, which with all
their peculiar excellences can hardly be claimed
as masterpieces of the art of story-telling. As a
dramatist he had great dramatic moments ; but
the element of artificiality which goes with all
dramatic writing, the power of welding facts to the

K

requirements of a rule-bound art, failed him. Moreover, he stood under another disadvantage—already referred to in these pages — the essentially untragic nature of his mind, which effectually prevented him writing an undiluted tragedy. His calm optimism did not allow him to cultivate that "sense for the cruel" which he appraised as the tragic quality in his friend Schiller's genius. "Without an active, pathological interest I have never succeeded in working out any tragic situation, and I have therefore rather avoided than sought out such situations." To say that Goethe was supreme as a lyric poet is only another way of saying that the peculiar strength of the German artistic genius lies in its power to give expression to the subjective ; the lyric has in all ages been the highest form of German literary excellence. And Goethe's lyric seems to sum up the qualities which we have learned to associate with the German lyric. It has the immediateness and direct truth of expression of the best popular lyric poetry—and the Germans have always regarded the folksong as an ideal to be striven for ; and, as in the folksong, there is in Goethe's poetry the thinnest possible veil between the emotion and its expression ; that expression has the instinctive justness of word and tone, which in an unconscious way the best folksongs attain ; it eliminates with no less sure an

instinct all that is merely of the intellect, that does
not fall within the legitimate sphere of lyric expression. But these are qualities that are true of all great
German lyric poetry, and of any great lyric poetry ;
and it is difficult to say wherein the peculiar differentiating qualities of Goethe's genius consist. The
lyric, like the diamond, is most precious when it is
freest from colour, from individual characteristics.
In the fact that Goethe instinctively selected the
right means to his end, lay his power. No singer
excelled him in the power of crystallising fleeting
emotions into thoughts and words and music. Other
German poets have been able to interpret the
spiritual in terms of the plastic, but their plastic
has rarely been plastic enough, or occasionally,
as in the case of Heine, it has gone to the opposite
extreme of excessive plasticity ; Goethe always
knew how to maintain the golden mean. To say,
again, that Goethe's lyric is essentially a lyric of
nature is no differentiating characteristic ; for that
feature is common to all the German lyric poets
from Klopstock onwards. But whereas Eichendorff
attuned his emotions to the voices of the forest,
Heine his to the music of the sea, and Lenau's
pessimistic soul found itself reflected in the Hun-
garian pusta, Nature with all her manifold voices
echoes through Goethe's lyric poetry. There is a
bigness and a universality about his lyric genius

K*

before which that of these other poets seems small
and personal.

A tribute to Goethe's many-sided personality is the
metamorphosis which the estimate of it has under-
gone in succeeding generations in Germany, France
and England. One might put side by side the
wrapt and adoring attitude of the early Romanticists
—who had as unclear an idea of Goethe as they
had of Raphael—with the open dislike of " Young
Germany " ; or the pessimistically coloured portraits of him in the Germany of the sixties with the
optimistic portraits of the nineties. The Goethe
of France, again, has never been the Goethe of
Germany ; and France, too, saw him in her different
periods at different angles. And in England we
have had the widest deviations from the essentially
Romantic, " renunciatory " Goethe of Carlyle, to
the " apostle of culture " of Matthew Arnold.

The Victorian portrait of Goethe was in the main
a moralist's one; he interested us less then as a poet
than as a teacher. But we can hardly revert nowadays to that old standpoint; we have come to realise
that it is no business of the supreme artist to teach.
At the same time it may be said in defence of that
opinion that Goethe was more than the supreme
artist ; much of his activity lay in fields where
teaching is the main object. Our change of attitude
lies rather in the fact that the lessons the generation

of sixty years ago drew from his works are no longer vital lessons to us, who, in our practical life, have to face other intellectual problems than they. Goethe was a leader to a generation which stood, like himself, on the brink of a new era ; and that generation naturally sought guidance from him as to what attitude they should take to the new problems. But the world has not developed as Goethe believed it would develop ; society has refused to march forward by such undevious ways, and on such clearly marked-out lines to a golden age of contented socialism, as were foreshadowed in the *Wanderjahre*. Man, on the contrary, finds it as hard to-day to be happy and contented with his lot as in the old unregenerate days. Science and philosophy have ceased to walk amiably hand in hand, as they did in the first thirty years of the nineteenth century. We have passed through collectivism and optimism to pessimism and individualism ; and we have swung back again to optimism. Literature has been romantic and realistic by turns ; above all, instead of that growing community of ideas, that realisation of the " world literature " to which Goethe looked so confidently forward, we have progressed on diametrically opposite lines. A new individualism has taken possession of the nations, the Romantic individualism which Goethe but dimly grasped has become the all-pervading and all-powerful idea of the last hundred years. The individual life and poetry of the little nations of Europe have developed in direct defiance of the cosmopolitan principles of " world literature " ; barriers of nationality, in taste, in art, in literature, in ideas, have been set up, which neither steam nor electricity has been able to break down. Goethe could obviously have had no presentiment of this development, so different is it from that cosmopolitan community of thought which dominated the Europe in which he lived.

These things militate against Goethe's present-day influence ; but to the individual man he still appeals with his pristine force ; for the problem of the individual life is, more or less, the same in all ages. Whatever we may say to the futility, or even shallowness, of Goethe's metaphysics ; however vague and elusive his religious thought may be ; however transient and unjustified by later developments his social and political theories, we have still to say that no thinker of modern times has spoken so wisely and with such finality on the conduct of the personal life as Goethe. And our own Carlyle, with his strong moralising bias, recognised this as no other of Goethe's contemporaries, even in Germany. Goethe's writings are thus still, at the beginning of the twentieth century, a valuable guide to the practical wisdom of the individual life.

But, in saying so, we must recognise frankly that

Goethe's articles of faith rest on positive, optimistic presuppositions, which are no longer universally accepted ; the golden rule of human conduct, as enunciated in the poetic allegory of *Faust*, is the last and highest development of optimistic thinking in Europe, which began with Leibniz and ripened in the confident common sense of the " Aufklärung." This is the historical position of Goethe's thinking, and in its definite historical position lies its limitations.   No dogmas are for all time, and even before Goethe's career had run to its end, a new thinker had arisen in Europe who voiced an entirely different faith, built up on a supposition in direct antagonism to Goethe's practical ethics.   The nineteenth century rose up on a foundation, not of rationalistic optimism, but of romantic pessimism ; and on this new basis it had to formulate its ethic principles anew.   " Entsagung " became, not what it was to Goethe, merely a pattern of a darker hue in the fabric of life, but synonymous with " Entbehren," the one reality, the bedrock of our whole morality. With this change of attitude new problems of the individual and social life arose, which Goethe's optimistic humanism and socialism could not solve. But the pessimistic phase of Schopenhauer—of Grillparzer and Lenau, of Leopardi and Wagner— had in turn to pass ; and the pendulum has swung back again to a healthier outlook on life, which, although little in harmony with Goethe's social ideals, at least recognises and welcomes his magnificent individualism and his healthy maxims for the guidance of the individual life. No doubt this again will pass, for nowhere is finality; but it at least means for us a vital tie between Goethe, the ripest product of the European " Aufklärung," and our own time. Goethe has still the power, in Carlyle's phrase, to " free us from Unbelief," to lead us back to a faith in ourselves, to help us to grapple with doubt and despair, to teach us :

> Uns vom Halben zu entwöhnen,
> Und im Ganzen, Guten, Schönen,
> Resolut zu leben.

INDEX

www.ingramcontent.com/pod-product-compliance
Ingram Content Group UK Ltd.
Pitfield, Milton Keynes, MK11 3LW, UK
UKHW042145280225
455719UK00001B/107

9 781107 401853